Next Level Thinking

10 Powerful Thoughts for a Successful and Abundant Life

Joel Osteen

New York   Nashville

ALSO BY JOEL OSTEEN

All Things Are Working for Your Good

Daily Readings from All Things Are Working for Your Good

Blessed in the Darkness

Blessed in the Darkness Journal

Blessed in the Darkness Study Guide

Break Out!

Break Out! Journal

Daily Readings from Break Out!

Every Day a Friday

Every Day a Friday Journal

Daily Readings from Every Day a Friday

Fresh Start

Fresh Start Study Guide

I Declare

I Declare Personal Application Guide

Next Level Thinking

Next Level Thinking Study Guide

The Power of I Am

The Power of I Am Journal

The Power of I Am Study Guide

Daily Readings from The Power of I Am

Think Better, Live Better

Think Better, Live Better Journal

Think Better, Live Better Study Guide

Daily Readings from Think Better, Live Better

With Victoria Osteen

Our Best Life Together

Wake Up to Hope Devotional

You Can, You Will

You Can, You Will Journal

Daily Readings from You Can, You Will

Your Best Life Now

Your Best Life Begins Each Morning

Your Best Life Now for Moms

Your Best Life Now Journal

Your Best Life Now Study Guide

Daily Readings from Your Best Life Now

Scriptures and Meditations for Your Best Life Now

Starting Your Best Life Now

Next Level Thinking

FaithWords
Hachette Book Group
1290 Avenue of the Americas, New York, NY 10104
faithwords.com
twitter.com/faithwords

Originally published in hardcover and ebook by FaithWords in October 2018
First trade paperback edition: September 2019

FaithWords is a division of Hachette Book Group, Inc. The FaithWords name and logo are trademarks of Hachette Book Group, Inc.

The publisher is not responsible for websites (or their content) that are not owned by the publisher.

The Hachette Speakers Bureau provides a wide range of authors for speaking events. To find out more, go to www.hachettespeakersbureau.com or call (866) 376-6591.

Literary development: Lance Wubbels Literary Services, Bloomington, Minnesota

Library of Congress Control Number: 2018944025

ISBNs: 978-1-5460-2597-9 (trade paperback), 978-1-5460-2595-5 (ebook)

Printed in the United States of America

LSC-C

10 9 8 7 6 5 4 3 2 1

CONTENTS

CHAPTER ONE

Be a Barrier Breaker

So often we let our environment, how we were raised, and other people's expectations of us set the limits for our life. We adapt to what's around us. If you take an oak tree seed and plant it in a two-foot pot, that oak tree will never become what it was created to be if you leave it in the pot—not because there's something wrong with the seed, but because of the environment that it's in. It's so easy to just fit in, to go with the crowd, to be like everyone else. But God didn't create you to be average. He created you to stand out, to go beyond the norm, to leave your mark on this generation. You have seeds of greatness on the inside. You're supposed to go further than the people who raised you. You're supposed to live better, be more successful, and set a new standard. You may be in an environment where people have addictions, low self-esteem, depression, and poverty. You can't stop that. But here's the key: Don't let that become normal in your thinking. If you accept that as who you are, it will keep you from your destiny.

The Scripture speaks of how we are *in* the world, but we are not *of* the world. You may be *in* a limited environment, but you don't have to be *of* it. Don't let that environment get in you. If you see struggle, lack, and poverty long enough, your mind can become conditioned to thinking, *This is who I am. I'll always struggle. I'll never have enough.* No, that's where you are, that's not who you are. That may be what's been normal. The good news is, you're a barrier breaker. You have the power, the favor, the talent, and the ability to break out and go further. God breathed His life into you. He calls you the head and not the tail. Don't let your mind become conditioned for mediocrity. Don't let that change who you really are.

Sometimes people will try to put us in a box. They'll tell us such things as, "You can't start that business. You don't have the resources. You'll never afford a nice place to live, never get well, never meet the right person." Because their thinking is limited, they'll try to put their limitations on you. You have to put your foot down and say, "I refuse to be mediocre because people around me are mediocre. I refuse to be addicted, depressed, and have low expectations. I know that I'm a barrier breaker. I'm going to set a new standard."

It starts in your thinking. Nothing will change until you make up your mind that you are not going to accept mediocrity. Why don't you take the limitations off yourself? You have so much potential. Break out of that box and try something new. The enemy would love to keep that potential from ever coming out. He'll use bad breaks, negative comments, people, and circumstances to try to keep you from believing in yourself, from believing that you can rise to the next level. Many people have let their mind become con-

Nothing will change until you make up your mind that you are not going to accept mediocrity.

ditioned to thinking they've reached their limits, they're just average, they'll never do anything great. What's happened? Instead of breaking out, they've adapted to their environment.

Take the Limitations Off

I saw a study that was done with fleas. Researchers put fleas in a container and then put a lid on the top. The fleas immediately tried to jump out, but they hit the lid again and again. Before long they realized they were stuck. At one point the researchers removed the lid, but, much to their surprise, the fleas didn't try to jump out anymore. They had hit that lid so many times that they had become conditioned to thinking they couldn't get out. Even though the lid was off, they didn't even try.

Sometimes, as with these fleas, because of the environment we're in, the times we've tried and failed, and what people have told us, we've become conditioned to thinking, *I can't do anything great. I'll never accomplish my dream. I'll never get back in shape.* It might not have happened in the past, you might have tried and hit that lid a few times, but can I tell you the lid is coming off? It's time to try again. You were not created to live contained, to get stuck. Recondition your mind.

That's what happened to a friend of mine. He got off to a rough start in life. He grew up in the projects, was very poor, and had almost no guidance. His father wasn't in his life, and his mother had her own struggles. Because of this poor home situation, he was labeled by the state as a "child at risk." From the time he was a little boy, that phrase had played over and over in his mind. It had become ingrained in his thinking: *There's no future for me. I'm a child at risk.* He continued to go downhill, getting into trouble, doing what the rest of the crowd was doing. Everyone around him was defeated, depressed, and addicted. He fit right in. He adapted to his environment. Your life is going to follow your thoughts. He believed he was at risk, and he became at risk. If you believe you've reached your limits, you have. If you believe you'll never get well, you won't. Because your mind has become conditioned with limitations, it will keep you from your highest potential.

You have to be bold and get rid of the thoughts that are holding you back. You may not see how you can do it in your own ability, but you're not on your own. You have the most powerful force in the universe breathing in your direction. God created you to rise higher, to break barriers of the past, to overcome bad habits, and to be free from generational curses. People may have labeled you at risk, average, less than, but God labels you well able, equipped, anointed, creative, a masterpiece. The good news is that people don't determine your destiny; God does. What they said about you, the environment you're in now, and how you were raised cannot keep you from your purpose. God has already taken into account every detail of your life—every bad break, every negative comment, how you were raised, what somebody did or didn't do. He's factored that all into His plan. If you stay in faith, instead of holding you back, it will propel you forward. Instead of defeating you, it will make you stronger. God knows how to take what was meant for your harm and use it to your advantage.

One day this young man got into trouble at school and was sent to the school counselor. She tried to reason with him, but he wouldn't listen. However, she wouldn't give up. She kept on trying and trying. Finally he said to her, "Why are you even bothering with me? I'll never do anything great. I've been told my whole life I'm a child at risk." She looked him in the eyes and said, "Listen to me: you are not a child at risk; you are a child at possibility." When he heard that, something ignited on the inside. He sat up in his chair and said to her, "What do you mean 'at possibility'?" She said, "You are full of poten- tial. You are smart, you are talented. There's so much you can become."

> *"Listen to me: you are not a child at risk; you are a child at possibility."*

His whole life, he'd heard just the opposite. His mind had become conditioned to thinking, *I'll never get out of the projects. I'll never be successful.* That day a stronghold was broken in his thinking. He recondi- tioned his mind.

Today, this young man owns his own business and is very successful. Plus, he goes around to schools and speaks to other students who are considered to be at risk. He tells them what that counselor told him: "You're not at risk; you're at possibility." As it was with my friend, people around you may accept mediocrity. They may be fine with being average, having little goals, working at an "okay" job. But don't let that spirit rub off on you. That's not who you are. You're the exception. You're a barrier breaker. You are not limited by your education, by how you were raised, by that environment. God has destined you to rise higher. He's destined you to go to the next level.

Become a Barrier Breaker

This is what happened with my father. He grew up in a very poor family on a cotton farm in Paris, Texas, during the Great Depression. At Christmastime, his family was the one that received the Christmas basket that went to the poorest family in the school. He was never allowed to drink a full glass of milk, because they couldn't afford it. They could only have a fourth of a glass, and they'd pour water in it to make it last longer. But when he was seventeen years old, my dad was the first one in the family to give his life to Christ, and he also made another major decision about his future. He told me, "Joel, I decided on that day that my children would never be raised in the poverty and lack that I was raised in." He changed his mind. The people around him were good people, but they were limited. Their minds had become conditioned to accept not having enough, to always struggle and lack. The problem is that if you accept it as your way of life, you won't do anything about it. It's easy to get comfortable with mediocrity and just adapt to your environment.

But when he was a teenager, my father felt something

stirring on the inside. It was those seeds of greatness. All the circumstances of his life said he was stuck. He'd have to stay on the farm and pick cotton the rest of his life. But instead of adapting to that environment, his attitude was, *This is not my destiny. I can rise above this. I refuse to live in mediocrity, wearing hand-me-downs, receiving the Christmas basket. I know I have seeds of greatness. I have potential. I have creativity. The Most High God breathed life into me.* As a teenager, he left the farm. He had to hitchhike to do it, but he went out and started ministering in the jails, in senior citizens' homes, and in schools, making a difference wherever he went. He broke the curse of poverty in our family and took us to a new level. He was a barrier breaker. He knew he was made for more.

Instead of just fitting into your environment and being like everyone else, why don't you start seeing yourself as a barrier breaker, as the exception? You're supposed to stand out. You're supposed to rise higher. Maybe everyone in your family is depressed except you. You broke out. You're happy. You're full of joy. Everyone is addicted except you. You're free. You're clean. You're helping others. Everyone is struggling, can't make ends meet, and can't get ahead except you.

You're blessed. Good breaks are chasing you down. Opportunities are looking for you. Your gifts and talents are coming out in greater ways. Why is that? You're the exception. You're not arrogant, you don't think you're better than someone else, but you have a quiet confidence, knowing that you were made for more.

If my father had accepted that poverty and a limited education was his lot in life, I wouldn't be where I am today. Are you accepting things that are less than God's best? Have you adapted to a limited environment? You have big dreams in your heart. You know there's a new business in you, a management position, a book, a better house, but you're doing as well as your friends. You've gone as far as your family has gone in the past. No, don't settle there. Break out of that mold. Nothing will be sadder than to come to the end of life and realize what we could have become if we had just lived with an at-possibility mind-set instead of an at-risk mentality.

> *Are you accepting things that are less than God's best?*

Get Rid of the Excuses

A couple of years before my dad went to be with the Lord, we drove back to his hometown. Daddy wanted to reminisce and show me where he had grown up. We went out onto the land where his farm used to be. The house was no longer there, but we found the well, and he showed me where he used to pick cotton, where he went to school. Before we left the town, we drove around to see if we could find any of his friends. We pulled up to a very run-down house that didn't even look livable. Really, it was nothing more than a shack. There was this older gentleman sitting on the front porch, not wearing a shirt, just killing time. My father went up and said, "I'm John Osteen. Are you So-and-so?" Yes, it was his friend. They hadn't seen each other in over sixty years. This man invited us inside, and the place was very dilapidated. There were buckets on the floor to catch the water leaks from the ceiling, and the broken windows were boarded up. Later we went around and found several of my father's other friends. They were all in the same situation—extreme poverty, defeat, mediocrity.

They were good people, but it hit me how little they had accomplished in their lives. They had made the mistake of accepting the limitations they were born into and then adapting to their environment. One man told how he'd worked a little here and there, worked down at the boat docks and at other odd jobs, barely making it through the years. Another man had been laid off his job twenty-eight years earlier and said he was not able to find any more work, so he lived off handouts, with no goals, no dreams, no resources. Now they were at the end of their lives, having never tapped into their potential.

That day made such an impression upon me. I thought about how my father was raised in the same environment. He came out of the same mold, the same Depression, the same poverty, the same school, but Daddy went on to touch the world and pastored great churches. He made a difference with his life. I saw firsthand what would have happened if my father had accepted the life of defeat he was born into. If he had not put his foot down and said, "I might have been born into mediocrity, but I am not settling here," if he had not reconditioned his mind, he would have been sitting right there with the rest of those men.

Don't go through life and miss your destiny. You weren't created to get stuck, to settle and stay at the same place year after year. You were created to excel. There is potential in you right now just waiting to come out. You have gifts that will cause new doors to open, talent that will bring new opportunities. Get rid of low expectations. Quit making excuses to settle where you are. You may be in a limited environment that includes dysfunction, addictions, and depression. The good news is, you don't have to stay there. That's not your destiny. Somebody

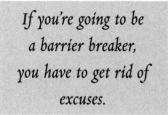

If you're going to be a barrier breaker, you have to get rid of excuses.

may have labeled you "at risk," but the Creator of the universe labels you "at possibility." You've gone as far as your family and your friends—that's good, but don't settle there. You're the exception. You're supposed to go further. Dare to take some steps of faith. Life is flying by. You don't have ten years to wait around. The odds may be against you, but the Most High God is for you. His favor on your life will cause you to go where you could not go on your own. If you're going to be a barrier breaker, you have to get rid of excuses.

Defy the Odds

I read about an eight-year-old boy who grew up in Kansas in the early 1900s. During the winter, he and his brother would go to school early to light the wood fire in the large potbellied stove in the classroom so that it would be warm when the rest of the students arrived. But one day someone accidentally put gasoline in the kerosene container he used to start the wood on fire. The next morning, when he lit the match, there was a huge explosion. His brother was killed instantly. The teacher came running and found this little boy unconscious, with the lower half of his body burned beyond recognition. She pulled him out of the fire thinking he was dead, but somehow he had survived. He'd lost all the flesh on his knees and shins and all the toes on his left foot. His mother was told that if he did make it, he would be crippled, never able to walk again, and the doctors recommended amputating his legs. But this little boy was a fighter. Against all odds, he survived. He made up his mind he was not only going to walk again, but he told everyone that one day he would run again. His favorite Scripture was found in Isaiah 40: "They that wait upon the

Lord will renew their strength. They will run and not be weary, they will walk and not faint." As an eight-year-old boy, he had a spirit of faith. He believed that he could defy the odds.

Months later he was sent home from the hospital with no movement in his legs. The doctors advised his parents to massage his legs to stretch the muscles and try to restore some suppleness to his lower limbs, which was incredibly painful because of the scar tissue. Every day his mother would take him outside in the wheelchair so he could get some sunshine. One afternoon when she wasn't watching, he grabbed on to the picket fence and pulled himself up. Stake by stake, he began to drag himself along. He did this day after day, teaching himself how to walk again. They didn't have physical therapy for him to go to; he was his own physical therapist. Two years after the accident, he stood up for the first time. Not long after that, he was not only walking, he began to run and became extremely fast. In college, on the track team, he won so many medals he became known as the Kansas Flyer. In 1934, Glenn Cunningham, the young man who had been told he'd never walk again, broke the world record in the mile run.

If you're going to be a barrier breaker, you have to get rid of excuses. Quit thinking about what you didn't get, what you can't do, how the odds are against you. You and God are a majority. You have what you need. You're a barrier breaker. You can defy the odds. You can beat the cancer, you can break the addiction, you can start the new business. You can go further than the experts have told you. As Glenn did, you have to recondition your mind. Instead of dwelling on all the negative things people have said about you, dwell on what God says about you: "I will run and not be weary." Instead of "You can't break that addiction," say "I can do all things through Christ. Whom the Son sets free is free indeed." Instead of "Oh, man, you've reached your limits. This is not for you today," declare that "the path of the righteous gets brighter and brighter. God's plans for me are for good and not evil, to give me a future and a hope." Nothing will happen until you change your mind. Glenn could have lain in bed thinking, *Wow, too bad for me. I lost my*

> *Instead of dwelling on all the negative things people have said about you, dwell on what God says about you.*

legs. I'll never do anything great. But if he had, we wouldn't be talking about him today.

Are there strongholds keeping you back? Have you adapted to an environment and let what people have said about you set the limits for your life? God is saying, "This is a new day. You're a barrier breaker. I'm going to take you further faster than you've imagined. I'm going to help you set a new standard. You're going to defy the odds." Now do your part. Let this seed take root in your spirit. Don't talk yourself out of it. Get in agreement with God.

Stir Up Seeds of Greatness

For years, experts said that no one would ever be able to run a mile in under four minutes. They studied the human body and thought it would collapse under that much pressure. Scientists said it was not only dangerous to try, but it was literally impossible. But a young man named Roger Bannister didn't believe the negative reports. He didn't let his mind become conditioned to thinking it couldn't be done. In May 1954, he made history by running a mile in under four minutes. What's interesting is that forty-six days later, someone else broke the four-minute mile. Within ten years, 336 people had run the mile in under four minutes' time. It hadn't happened in all the previous years of track and field history, and now it was happening all the time. Why was that? The barrier was broken in people's minds. For years runners had believed what the experts said. They were convinced in their own thinking that it couldn't happen. Once that barrier was removed, they were able to do things that seemed impossible. Has your mind become conditioned to thinking you can't accomplish your dreams, you can't get well, you'll never break that addiction? If you'll do as Roger did and recondition your mind, start thinking better, believing that you're a can-do person, knowing that you have seeds of greatness, you too will break barriers that you thought were impossible.

And here's the beauty: When you break a barrier, you make it easier for those who come after you. You're paving the way for your children, for your relatives. That's what it means to set a new standard. That's what my dad did. When he broke that curse of poverty, he took our family to a new level. Because he broke that barrier, I was able to start much further along. When my dad went to be with the Lord, he left us with an eight-thousand-seat auditorium. I could have settled there and thought, *This is okay. I'm doing as well as my parents.* But I did what I'm asking you to do. I stirred up my gifts and said, "God, I know I'm not supposed to stay at the same level as my parents." I took a step of faith, and God opened the door to the former Compaq Center, which is several times larger than our former facility. That's the way it's supposed to be. God is a progressive God. He wants every generation to increase.

> *When you break a barrier, you make it easier for those who come after you.*

There was a young man in the Scripture named Hezekiah who was raised in a very dysfunctional home. His father was King Ahaz of Judah, who set up idols for the people to worship. He was a very hard king and cruel to the people. Because he didn't honor God, the nation went downhill and became very poor. Five different armies came against Judah, and Judah lost every battle. The place was decimated. You would think that Ahaz would have learned his lesson, turned to God, asked for His help, but it was just the opposite. He closed the doors of the temple and began to sell off sacred treasures. Hezekiah was raised in this environment of compromise, defeat, and mediocrity. He could have turned out like his dad; he could have adapted to that environment. But Hezekiah understood this principle. When he became king, the first thing Hezekiah did, before repairing the roads or getting the economy going, was to reopen the temple. He turned the nation back toward God.

His father chose to compromise and to push people down, but Hezekiah's attitude was, *I might have been born into mediocrity, but I'm not settling here. I'm going to put an end to this generational curse, and I'm going to start a generational blessing.* Hezekiah was a barrier breaker. You may be in some kind of limited environment. If Hezekiah were here today, he would tell you, "You don't have to stay there." How you start is not important. How you finish is what matters. Do yourself and your family a favor. Break out of that mold. Don't pass negative things down to the next generation. You can be the difference maker. You can be the one who sets your family on a course to honoring God, a course of blessing, favor, and victory.

I'm asking you to recondition your mind. Get rid of strongholds that are keeping you back. You're not at risk; you're at possibility. Stir up your seeds of greatness. Be a barrier breaker. If you do this, I believe and declare God is going to breathe on your life in a new way. You're going to go beyond barriers of the past, overcome obstacles, and accomplish dreams. You're going to become everything God created you to be.

CHAPTER TWO

You Are Fully Loaded

When God created you, He put in you everything you need to fulfill your destiny. God is a strategic God. He's not random. He didn't just create you and say, "Let's see what he can do. Let's see what happens." God is precise. He's intentional, down to the smallest detail, and when He laid out the plan for your life, He studied it carefully. He thought about what you would need, and what it would take to get you there, then He matched you with your world. He gave you the talent you need, the creativity, the strength. You're the right size, and you have the right looks, the right personality, and the right family. You didn't get shortchanged. You are fully loaded and completely equipped for the race that's been designed for you.

Now quit wishing you were something different: "If I had a better personality, I could do something great," "If I came from a different family," "If I weren't so small." Have a new perspective. If you needed to be taller, God would've made you taller. If you needed a different personality, He would've given you one. If you needed to be another nationality, you would be another nationality. God doesn't make mistakes. You're not faulty. You have been fearfully and wonderfully made.

When God created the universe, when He flung stars into space, He said, "That was good." When He created the mountains, oceans, and sunsets, He said, "That was good." When He made the animals, lions, eagles, and butterflies, He said, "That was good." But when God created you, when He saw how magnificent you are, how strong, how attractive, and how talented you are, He said, "That was *very* good." He didn't say the solar system was very good. He didn't say the Rocky Mountains were very good. The only time He used "very good" is when He created you.

In Ephesians, He calls you "a masterpiece." When the Creator of the universe says, "You are very good," that means you are just right! Now don't go around feeling shortchanged, as though somehow you're lacking, you didn't get enough, you can't do what others can do. If you didn't get what somebody else has, that means you don't need it. Quit comparing yourself to others and run your race. Be who God created you to be. You are an original. You have something to offer the world that nobody else has. Let your gifts shine. Show your talent, your personality, your style. We don't need an imitation. We don't need a copy. We need the original you.

When you want what somebody else has, when you wish you had their looks, their talent, their personality, the truth is, if you had it, it wouldn't be a blessing. It would be a burden. It wasn't designed for you. The reason it works for them is because it fits them. They're walking in their anointing. You are not anointed to be somebody else. As long as you're trying to be like them, you'll be frustrated. The anointing on your life is to be who God called you to be. Be confident in what you have. Next level thinking says you have the right looks, the right talent, and the right personality. It might not be what somebody else has, but you're not running their race.

> *The anointing on your life is to be who God called you to be.*

Nobody Can Beat You at Being You

When my father went to be with the Lord, he had pastored Lakewood for forty years. I had been behind the scenes, doing the television production, and when he died I had ministered only one time, but I knew I was supposed to step up and pastor the church. However, I thought I needed to be like my dad. After all, people had come to hear him for years, and I knew that was what they were expecting from me. For the first few months I tried to preach like my dad and lead like my dad, but it was a struggle. I had good intentions. I wanted to honor my father, but there's no grace on your life to be somebody else. One day I read in the book of Acts, "David fulfilled his purpose for his generation," and I heard something down inside say, "Joel, your father fulfilled his purpose. Now quit trying to be like him, and go out and fulfill your purpose." It was as though a stronghold was broken in my mind that took me to the next level. I realized that I'm free to be me. I quit trying to imitate my father, and I stepped into my own anointing. That's when the ministry began to grow.

I've learned that it's easy to be me. I don't have to pretend. I don't have to perform. That takes all the pressure off. I can relax and just be myself. When you're comfortable with who you are, when you're not trying to impress people, you're not trying to be something that you're not, then your own uniqueness will come out. You'll be more creative. Your talent will come out in greater ways. The right people will show up. Why? Because you've stepped into the anointing on your life. Be you. You are powerful when you're you. Here's a key: Nobody can beat you at being you. You can be a better you than anybody in the world. You have an advantage. You've been anointed to be you.

When I minister, I'm more conversational, and I don't get real loud and excited. But growing up, I used to think that to be an effective minister you had to be loud and forceful and dynamic. I have minister friends who are that way, and they are very powerful. That's who they are. But I've learned that when you're who you are, you can be quiet and be powerful. You can be small and be powerful. You can be behind the scenes and be powerful. The whole key is to be you, because when you're you, you activate your anointing. There's a favor, a blessing, a grace that is unique to your life.

Too often when we see someone who's more talented, more successful, more blessed, there's a tendency to be envious and think, *Why can't I do that? I want what they have.* If we're not careful, before long we'll be competing with them, trying to outperform them, outdress them, outdrive them, outwork them. The problem is that you're competing with someone who's not in your race. Your race is specifically for you. You're not in competition with your friends, your neighbors, your coworkers, or your siblings. The only competition you have is with yourself, to be the best that you can be.

> *The only competition you have is with yourself, to be the best that you can be.*

I realize that I can't preach like Bishop Jakes, I can't sing like Steve Crawford, and I can't do surgery like my brother, Paul, but I can encourage someone. I can inspire a few people. I can smile. I'm good at that!

Don't get distracted trying to keep up with someone whom you were never supposed to keep up with. When you understand you are fully loaded for the race that's been designed for you, instead of competing with people, you'll celebrate them. The right attitude is, *They may have something that I don't, but that's okay. I'm not running their race. I'm equipped for my destiny.*

Run Your Own Race

In the Scripture, King Saul lost the throne when he saw David rising higher and gaining more influence than him. Instead of celebrating David, he became jealous. When people started singing, "Saul has defeated thousands," he was happy. "People are celebrating me. I've done something great!" But then the song continued, "And David has defeated tens of thousands." Saul couldn't handle anybody being in front of him. He didn't realize they weren't in the same race. He wasn't competing with David. If Saul had been happy for David, he wouldn't have missed his destiny.

When we start competing with people, we get distracted, we lose focus, and before long we're wasting time on things that are not moving us toward our purpose. Someone has said, "Successful people are so focused on their own goals that they don't have time to look around to see what everybody else is doing." Run your race, and when somebody passes you by, don't be intimidated. Be inspired. If God did it for them, He can do it for you. But if you can't celebrate people who are further along than you, you'll never get to where they are. You have to pass the test of being happy for people who have passed you up, because there will be the tendency to be jealous, to start finding fault and being critical, saying, "Well, they don't deserve it. They're not that talented anyway. Let me tell you some bad things I heard about them." Don't fall into that trap. God's showing them favor doesn't mean He's not going to show you favor. Be happy for them.

When you see someone who's blessed, who's rising higher, it's easy to think, *Well, they've just had a lot of good breaks.* What you might not realize is that the favor on their life didn't come without pain. The promotion didn't come without struggles, without them fighting off discouragement, without them pressing forward when they felt like giving up. You don't know what it took for them to get where they are. Sometimes we come in at the end of the movie. We see everything working out. They're happy, blessed, successful. What we didn't see was the middle—the tears, the lonely nights, the struggles. Be big enough to celebrate what God is doing in their life. Don't be a Saul. Don't miss your destiny because you're sour that somebody passed you up. Their success is not

> *Don't be a Saul. Don't miss your destiny because you're sour that somebody passed you up.*

stopping what God wants to do in your life. God didn't use up all of His favor on them.

It's a test. Are you going to compete with them and spend all your energy trying to keep up, or are you going to celebrate what God has done? You can tell who your true friends are not by who comes when you fall and are down. When you make a mistake, people will feel sorry. They'll show up to help you. Your true friends are the ones who show up when you succeed. They celebrate when you're promoted. They're happy when God blesses you. They're high-fiving you when you move into that new house. You've heard the saying "It's lonely at the top." It's because not everybody can handle your success, and too often people get envious, jealous, critical. Let's pass this test. When somebody passes you by, give them a high five and keeping running your race. Don't look to the left or to the right. Keep being who God's made you to be.

One time I was out running through my neighborhood, and I saw a man running about a quarter
of a mile in front of me. I thought, *I'm going to
catch him.* I had about a mile to go before I needed
to turn off and go down my path. I picked up the
pace and started gaining on him and gaining on him,
and I was feeling great and thinking, *Look what I'm
doing!* Getting closer and closer, I finally passed him.
I beat him! He hadn't known we were racing, but I
felt good about it! About that time I realized I had
been so focused on catching him that I'd missed my
turn. I had to turn around and go back about six
blocks to where I was supposed to turn.

That's what happens when we start competing with
people. It's a distraction. We're running in a race that
we're not supposed to be in, competing with people who
many times don't even know it. If that man knew we
were racing, I'd probably still be trying to catch him. He
would've sped up! Don't get distracted. Run your race.

Know Who You Are and Who You're Not

In the Scripture, John the Baptist was baptizing people
and gaining a lot of attention. At one point the Jew-

ish leaders came and asked him if he was the Christ. Without missing a beat John said, "I am not the Messiah." It's important to know not only who you are, but to know who you're not. If you don't know this, you can spend your life trying to be something that you're not. John had no problem saying, "I am not the Messiah." He was saying, "I don't have to be the Messiah to feel good about myself. I'm content with who God made me to be."

If you're trying to be something you're not, you'll be frustrated. There's no grace for it. It will be a constant struggle, always like it's uphill. If Saul had understood this, he could have kept the throne. If he had accepted and said, "I am not David. He's defeated tens of thousands

> *If you're trying to be something you're not, you'll be frustrated. There's no grace for it.*

and done great things. I've defeated a thousand, and God has blessed me," it would have been a different story.

Most of the time we're happy until we start comparing. When Saul heard the numbers—"David defeated tens of thousands"—I can imagine him asking someone, "How many did they say David has defeated?" When they answered, "Tens of thousands," Saul's whole perspective changed. He was no longer content with his success. Now he was envious, jealous. He basically spent the rest of his life trying to be David. All he had to do was realize: "I am not David. God has blessed him in a different way."

We have to understand the sovereignty of God. It might not seem fair to us, and it doesn't always make sense to us, but God's ways are not our ways, and the Scripture talks about how God has given to every person different gifts, different talents, according to our own ability. Everyone doesn't get the same, but what He gave you is what you need to fulfill your destiny. Whether you're a Saul and you can defeat a thousand, or you're a David and you can defeat ten thousand, the right attitude is, *I'm going to take what God's given me and make the most of it.* Don't compete, don't compare, just run your race.

In the parable Jesus told of the talents in Matthew 25, the owner gave one man one talent, another man two talents, and another man five talents. It seems like if God was fair, He would have given them all the same number, but God is sovereign. He might give you five talents and give me two talents. He's God. I can complain about the two, try to compete with you and outperform you, but that doesn't change the fact that you still have five and I have two. A better approach is to say, "God, I recognize You are sovereign, and before You gave me these two talents, I didn't have any. So instead of complaining about the two and competing with the person who has five, I'm going to take these two talents and be the best that I can be."

It takes a mature person to recognize what you're not. Knowing what you're not will help you stay focused on becoming who you are, because there will always be pressures to be this, to be that, to be the other. Everyone will have opinions about you, but down in your heart you know who you are. You can't let the outside pressures and other people squeeze you into becoming something that you're not.

> *You can't let the outside pressures and other people squeeze you into becoming something that you're not.*

Don't Discount Your Gift

When I first started ministering, I was young and didn't have much experience, and I had a lot of people giving me their opinions. They told me how to lead the church, how to minister, what I should speak on. And sometimes it wasn't what they said, it was what they implied. I could feel the pressure to be who they wanted me to be. They were good people, but people didn't breathe life into you. People didn't lay out your plan and purpose. People didn't put gifts and talents on the inside. I was always respectful, but I was firm. When I heard a lot of their advice, I knew it wasn't what God had put in my heart, and I had to be bold and say, "I am not that. I am not that. I am not that. This is who I am."

You have to be strong. It's your destiny. When you come to the end of life, you're not going to answer to people. You're going to answer to God. People may mean well, they may love you, but if it doesn't bear witness in your spirit, you have to be bold and say, like John the Baptist, "That is not who I am."

Here's the key: you don't have to have a great gift for God to use you in a great way. You know what took David to the throne? It wasn't his leadership skills, his ability to write music, his personality, or his size. What promoted David was his gift of slinging a rock. He was good with a slingshot. When he was a teenager out in the shepherds' fields, he had spent hours practicing while he was caring for his father's sheep. He could have thought, *God, why didn't You give me an impressive gift? Why did You give me just one talent? I'm an expert with a slingshot. Big deal. That's never going to take me anyplace.* But if you'll be faithful with the gift you have, if you'll develop it, grow, learn, and get better, that gift will open doors to places you've never dreamed.

Don't discount your gift. It may seem small to you. Compared to others, it feels insignificant, but there is nothing ordinary about you. You have the fingerprints of God all over you. God made you in His own image. He crowned you with favor. You have royal blood flowing through your veins. Don't believe the lies: "There's nothing special about you." "You're not as talented as your brother." "You don't have a big personality like your friend." "You don't have the design skills that your coworker has."

> *There is nothing ordinary about you.*

Maybe you don't have what they have, but you do have a slingshot. There's something God has given you, and that slingshot may seem ordinary, but when God breathes on it, you'll defeat a giant twice your size, you'll be promoted beyond your talent, you'll go places where you didn't have the experience. You weren't next in line, but suddenly the door opened, suddenly the Compaq Center is yours, suddenly people are celebrating you.

Too often we look at others and think about how great they are. We put them on a pedestal, but God has put greatness in you. He's given you gifts, creativity, and dreams. He created you to leave your mark on this generation. You're not supposed to live and die and nobody knew you were here. There is something significant about you, something that will cause you to stand out to the point where, years from now, people will look back and say, "You made the world a better place." Stir up those gifts. Stir up that faith. Don't get so caught up in celebrating others that you don't recognize there's something in you to be celebrated.

It's Your Time to Be Celebrated

The prophet Jeremiah said, "Your word, O Lord, is like fire shut up in my bones." There is something shut up in you, something big that's about to be released—dreams, books, movies, inventions, businesses, ministries, potential that you haven't tapped into, gifts and talents that you hadn't known were there. You haven't seen them yet because it hasn't been the right time, but your season is coming. The good break, the promotion, the opportunity—it's on the way.

Now don't be surprised if there's opposition. That promotion may be disguised as Goliath. That giant looks as though it's there to stop you, but it's a setup. It's going to thrust you to the next level. You're going to discover what the slingshot was all about. It was a test. You proved your faithfulness. You did the right thing when nobody was watching. You kept a good attitude when it wasn't fair. You celebrated others when you could have been jealous. Now your time is coming. What's been shut up in your spirit is about to be released. It's going to be bigger, more rewarding, more fulfilling than you ever imagined. It's not going to come through your neighbor, through your cousin, through your boss, or through your pastor. It's going to come through you. It's your baby. It's your time to be celebrated.

This is what happened in the Scripture with Sarah. She and her husband, Abraham, were very old. Sarah had been barren her whole life and not able to have

> *One touch of God's favor will catapult you to the next level.*

children, but God said to Abraham in Genesis 17, "I will give Sarah a son. She will be the mother of nations. Kings of people will come out of her." Every circumstance said it was impossible. She was out in the desert, there were no fertility treatments or medical procedures, and she was ninety years old. Yet God said, "You have kings in you. You have nations in you." He was saying, "Sarah, what I put in you is more than you can imagine." God is saying the same thing to you: "There are kings in you. There is greatness in you. It's much bigger than what you think." Don't let circumstances talk you out of it. You may not see how it can work out. God has ways to do it that you've never thought of. One touch of God's favor will catapult you to the next level.

When Sarah heard this, it was so unbelievable that she laughed. She said, "Me, have a baby? I don't think so!" Even fifteen years earlier she had thought that if they were ever going to have a baby, it would have to come through somebody else, so she had tried to help God out. She had Abraham sleep with her maid, and they had a son. She was so excited and had said, "God,

You did what You said!" God replied, "Sarah, that is not the promised child. I didn't put the promise in somebody else. I put the promise in you." At ninety years old, against all odds, she became pregnant and gave birth to a son named Isaac.

What God has put in you, He's still going to bring to pass. You are pregnant with destiny. You are pregnant with greatness. It's not going to come through others. You're going to shine. You're going to excel. You're going to be promoted. You're going to be celebrated. You are fully loaded. You're not at a deficit. You're not lacking. You're full of potential, full of favor. As with Sarah, you may have been barren for a long time. You don't see how it can happen, but get ready. This is a new day. Things are changing in your favor. I believe and declare that what's been shut up in your spirit is being released. Dreams are being released, potential, promotion, healing, abundance, vindication, breakthroughs, and the fullness of your destiny, in Jesus' name.

CHAPTER THREE

The Odds Are for You

It's easy to go through life thinking of all the reasons why we can't be successful, why we won't get well, or why we'll never meet the right person. We look at our situations in the natural and think the odds are against us. I talked to a man who struggles with an addiction. He said, "Joel, my dad had this same addiction, and my grandfather struggled with it. The odds don't look too good for me." But as long as you think the odds are against you, you will get stuck where you are. You have the most powerful force in the universe breathing in your direction. God has crowned you with favor. He has armed you with strength for every battle. He wouldn't have allowed that difficulty if He wasn't going to turn it around and use it to your advantage. The odds may be against you, but the Most High God is for you, and He is a supernatural God. He parts Red Seas. He turns water into wine. He opens the eyes of the blind. Your circumstances may look impossible, but the God Who can do the impossible is working behind the scenes arranging things in your favor, turning negative situations around.

Since God is for you, that means the odds are for you. Don't go through life thinking, *Not me, Joel. I come from the wrong family. The odds are against me.* No, turn it around. *I've been born into a new family. My heavenly Father controls the universe. I have royal blood flowing through my veins.* When you know the odds are for you, you will put your shoulders back. You will carry yourself with confidence and expect to do great things. All through the day, this should be playing in our mind: "The odds are for me. I am destined to accomplish my dreams. I am destined to overcome this challenge. I am a child of the Most High God."

But don't be surprised when you find yourself in situations where it feels as though the odds are against you. You don't see a way out. There aren't any logical solutions. God puts you there on purpose so that when He turns it around, nobody will get the credit except Him. Everyone will know it is the hand of the Lord. When your circumstances seem impossible, instead of being discouraged and thinking, *God, why me?*, get ready. You're in perfect position for God to show out in your life and take you to the next level. He

> *Don't be surprised when you find yourself in situations where it feels as though the odds are against you.*

is setting you up to show His favor in amazing ways.

Setbacks Are Setups

This is what happened to a man in the Scripture named Gideon. The Midianites and two other armies came against him. They were about to attack the Israelites. Gideon sent word to his men to come and fight. Thirty-two thousand warriors showed up, but the enemy forces had one hundred and thirty-five thousand men. I can imagine Gideon was discouraged. He was outnumbered five to one, when God said to him, "You have too many men. If you defeat the Midianites, you will think you did it in your own strength." He instructed Gideon to let everyone who was afraid go home, and twenty-two thousand men left. Gideon nearly passed out. Two-thirds of his army went home. He didn't like these odds anymore. When he thought it couldn't get any worse, God said, "Gideon, you still have too many." He told him to eliminate even more men, and Gideon was finally left with only three hundred men to fight an army of over one hundred thousand. These odds seemed impossible. It looked as though Gideon would be wiped out. But what Gideon didn't realize was that God wasn't setting him back, He was setting him up. He was about to show out in Gideon's life.

Gideon and those three hundred men went to the enemy's camp in the middle of the night, blew their trumpets and let out a loud shout. The Midianites got confused in the darkness and began to fight among themselves. The Israelites defeated them, and they hardly had to lift a finger to do it. It had looked like a setback, but the truth was that God was setting Gideon up. He was putting him in position to show Himself strong.

When the odds seem like they're against you, and the obstacles look bigger, stronger, and more powerful, don't worry. As with Gideon, it is a setup. God is about to make things happen that you could never make happen. He is going to turn that situation around without you having to go to battle. He is going to heal you without the extensive treatment. He is going to promote you without all of the qualifications.

Keep the right perspective. Next level thinking says the odds are for you. You may feel like the underdog, but you and God are a majority. You don't need everyone to be for you. You don't have to have all the support and encouragement. You have the One Who matters. The Most High God is breathing in your direction.

> *Next level thinking says the odds are for you.*

Later, when the Israelites went to different cities, their armies would have usually attacked them. But the leaders said, in effect, "Gideon, we saw what your God did to the Midianites." They weren't afraid of Gideon. They were afraid of the God of Gideon. They knew the Lord was on his side.

God wants to give you victory to where people know the Lord is on your side. Maybe you didn't have the support growing up, the encouragement, and the stability. You should have been a statistic, but here you are, defying the odds, leaving your mark, going further than you ever dreamed. What happened? The

Lord is on your side. The medical report said you wouldn't make it, but here you are, strong, healthy, and whole. The Lord is on your side. Perhaps the odds said you would be addicted like your father, you would struggle like your grandfather, but here you are, free and clean. You broke the curse. You set a new standard. How could this be? The Lord is on your side.

Don't Let the Odds Fool You

When we were trying to acquire the former Compaq Center, every expert told us that we wouldn't get it, that the city wasn't going to let a church have it. On the surface, the odds were against us. But we understood this principle: When you don't see a way, when you feel outnumbered, when the giants look bigger and have more resources and more experience, that means God is up to something. As with Gideon, He is getting you in position to launch you to the next level. God made things happen that we could never make happen, and some of the same people who were against us, the same ones who said we would never get it, are our biggest supporters today.

One of the city council members who voted against us, a very vocal opponent, later said, "Joel, that was the biggest mistake of my political career. I watch you every Sunday. I bring people to your services. I don't know what I was thinking back then." I didn't tell him, but he was a part of the setup. God was using him to launch us forward.

That's what it says in the book of Exodus. "God caused Pharaoh to harden his heart so that He could bring great glory at the expense of Pharaoh." God had told Moses to go tell Pharaoh, "Let My people go." But God knew that Pharaoh wasn't going to let them go. He caused him to harden his heart. God was setting up the odds to be against the Israelites so He could show His favor. In a similar way, you may not like it that some people and circumstances have come against you; it wasn't fair, but it was ordained by God—not to stop you, not to defeat you, but so that God can show out in your life. Now quit complaining about what didn't work out and asking, "Why am I facing these giants?" If you will stay in faith, it's just a matter of time before God turns around those

> *The odds are against you for one reason—so God can bring great glory out of your life.*

obstacles that look like they are stopping you and uses them to push you forward. The odds are against you for one reason—so God can bring great glory out of your life. He wants to make you an example of His goodness.

Remember that when the three Hebrew teenagers, Shadrach, Meshach, and Abednego, wouldn't bow down to the king's golden idol, the king got so furious that he was going to have them thrown into a fiery furnace. He told his men to heat up the fire seven times hotter than normal. What was God doing? Making the odds even greater. God knew the fire wasn't going to burn them. He knew they weren't going to be harmed. He had them turn it up even hotter so it would become a greater miracle. When the three Hebrew teenagers came out of that fire without even the smell of smoke on their clothes, there wasn't any doubt that the Lord was on their side. In fact, this same king said, "Praise be to the God of Shadrach, Meshach, and Abednego."

When it feels like the odds are against you, the fire has been turned up seven times hotter, when Pharaoh won't let you go, and God took your army from thirty-two thousand to three hundred, don't panic. Don't fall apart. It's a setup. God is about to show out. He is about to make you a testimony. He is going to do something that people cannot deny. They are going to know the Lord is on your side.

I talked to a man who cut his hand and developed a severe infection. He tried for several days to tough it out and hoped that it would go away, but it kept getting worse. He started running a high fever. It got to the point where he couldn't eat. He finally passed out and was rushed to the emergency room unconscious. The doctors told his family that he had some type of toxic shock and there was only a 50 percent chance that he would live. They had to find the right antibiotic to treat him, and every hour that went by without the right treatment, his chance of survival went down 5 percent. If they didn't find something in the next few hours, the doctors said that he probably wouldn't make it, and if, somehow, he did survive, he would be in a vegetative state. Twelve hours went by, and they hadn't found the right antibiotic. One day later, still nothing. It was 264 hours later when they finally found the right treatment. He wasn't supposed to still be alive. He was told he would never be able to walk, talk, or function properly, but today he is perfectly healthy. You would never know anything was wrong.

God could have healed this man the first day. The doctors could have found the right treatment in the first few hours. That would have been a great miracle. But sometimes God will let the odds grow greater to where you don't see a way out, and then suddenly He will step in and make things happen that you could never make happen. Don't let the odds fool you. Don't let the fact that you don't see a way—the financial situation looks too far gone, you've tried to break that addiction for years—cause you to think it wasn't meant to be. No, get ready. This is a setup. This is not the time to give up. This is the time to stir your faith up. All through the day say, "Lord, thank You that You're bigger than this sickness, greater than this addiction, more powerful than these opponents." If you stay in faith, you are going to become a testimony like this man did. People are going to look at you and see that God's favor is on your life.

Something Even Better

In the Scripture, Mary and Martha sent word to their friend Jesus that their brother, Lazarus, was very sick. Jesus was in a different city, and they thought that

He would come right away and pray for Lazarus. They had seen Jesus heal people before. They knew that He could heal their brother. One day passed, and Jesus didn't show up. I am sure that Martha thought, *Jesus, where are You? What's taking You so long?* Another day went by, but still no sign of Jesus. Finally Lazarus died. When Jesus arrived at their house, Lazarus had been in the tomb for four days. Mary and Martha were so upset. They said, "Jesus, if You had been here, our brother would still be alive." The odds weren't that good when he was sick, but now that he was dead, they looked impossible. Lazarus was already wrapped up like a mummy in grave clothes. Against all apparent odds, Jesus went to the tomb, spoke to Lazarus and told him to come back to life, and Lazarus did! It was a great miracle.

Sometimes God will wait on purpose until the odds are way against you. You're ready to bury the dream, bury the promise, bury the relationship. You don't see a way it can work out. But God's ways are not our ways. Mary and Martha were praying for a healing, but God had

> *Mary and Martha were praying for a healing, but God had something better in store. He had a resurrection.*

something better in store. He had a resurrection. What you're tempted to give up on, you don't see how it can happen, maybe God is not going to do it the way you're thinking. Maybe He has something better for you.

We tried twice to buy property on which to build a new sanctuary. Both times the properties were sold out from under us. We couldn't find any more large tracts of land. I was discouraged. I didn't think we would ever have a bigger sanctuary. Then one day the Compaq Center suddenly became available. I was praying for a healing, but God had a resurrection, something better than I had ever dreamed.

The odds may be totally against you today, but can I tell you that God is totally for you. He has not brought you this far to leave you. Your circumstances may look dead. You've been asking and asking, but God didn't show up on time. Dare to trust Him. He has you in the palms of His hands. You may not see anything happening, but He is working behind the scenes, and when He speaks, dead things come back to life. He is not moved by the odds. When Jesus found out that Lazarus was dead, He didn't say, "Oh, man. I waited too long. What am I going to do now?" God controls the universe. The odds do not determine what He can and cannot do.

What's interesting is that most of the Jewish people who were very against Jesus believed that the spirit left the body three days after a person died. It wasn't a coincidence that Jesus waited until the fourth day to show up. He did this on purpose, so when He raised Lazarus, there wouldn't be any doubt about it. Sometimes God will let the odds become greater so not just you, but also your critics, your neighbors, your relatives, and your coworkers won't be able to deny what God has done. I love the fact that from that moment forward Lazarus became a testimony. Everywhere he went, he didn't have to say a word. People pointed at him. You can hear them whispering, "Look. There is that guy. He was dead. He is not supposed to be here." Lazarus defied the odds. He was a living testimony. That's what God wants to do for you, to show you His favor in such a way that people notice, that you stand out. You're going to become a living testimony.

The Odds Cannot Stop You

Are you letting the odds talk you out of your dreams, talk you out of your health, talk you out of your freedom? I know a young lady who applied for a scholarship

> *If you're letting the odds talk you out of stretching, out of dreaming, out of believing, you're going to miss the fullness of your destiny.*

at a prestigious university. Twenty-six hundred other students applied as well. The challenge was that there were only twelve scholarships available. Those odds were less than one half of one percent. She could have thought, *What's the use? There's no point in even trying. These are impossible odds.* Instead, she did what I am asking you to do. She dared to believe that God would open the doors that she was supposed to go through. It doesn't always happen the way we think. God knows what's best. But if you're letting the odds talk you out of stretching, out of dreaming, out of believing, you're going to miss the fullness of your destiny. If you can accomplish everything in your own strength, you don't need God's help. But when the odds are against you, and you don't see a way, you don't have the connections or the finances, you're too young or too old, that's when you have to dig your heels in and say, "God, I know these odds are no problem for You. I know this is a setup for You to show out." That's what this young lady did. Several months later she received a letter saying, "Congratulations. Out of twenty-six hundred applicants, you're one of the twelve that we have chosen."

Not long ago the lottery was at a record amount. I read that the odds of winning it were one in three hundred million. They used the example that if you laid pennies on the ground side by side from Seattle to Miami, and you marked one of those pennies with a special *X*, the chances of your winning that lottery were the same as your choosing that one special penny between Seattle and Miami. They were basically saying, "Forget about it. You're not going to win."

The book of Genesis talks about how God created the heavens and the earth. The word it uses for *creation* means that He made them out of nothing. Every expert would have said, "That's impossible. You don't have anything to work with. If You had skies, oceans, grass, and air, then maybe You could put it together and make something. But You can't do that with nothing." It's one thing to have odds of twelve in twenty-six hundred. That's not so great. It's another to have odds of one in three hundred million. That's very unlikely. But what about when the odds are zero in three hundred million, or zero in twenty-six hundred? It's impossible. There is no chance.

Here is how amazing God is: He started the universe with odds of zero. He had nothing to work with, no way in the natural, but God is not moved by the odds. He didn't check with Accounting and say, "I am about to create the stars, galaxies, and planets. I have nothing to work with. What are the odds of this happening?" Accounting would have said, "Zero. You have no materials, no resources." God would have said, "Thank you for your information. Now let there be light," and light would come shooting out at 186,000 miles a second.

God spoke worlds into creation. He didn't google it to see if it was possible. He didn't try to figure out a way. He is the way. He didn't try to open a door. He is the door. He doesn't check the odds to see if you can reach your destiny. He speaks and it becomes your destiny. God is not limited by your background, by how you were raised, by your education. He is all-powerful. He can take nothing and make something magnificent. Imagine what He can do with you. You are His prized possession. He breathed His life into you. You have the DNA of Almighty God. There may be odds against you in certain areas, but they cannot stop you. God has destined you to leave your mark. Don't let the odds discourage you. Don't let what you think is not going to happen talk you out of believing. Even if the odds are zero in a million, all God has to do is speak and the odds change in your favor.

> *Even if the odds are zero in a million, all God has to do is speak and the odds change in your favor.*

Your Time Is Coming

A friend of mine grew up in a very dysfunctional environment. His father wasn't around and his mother had mental disorders. When she wasn't in the psychiatric ward, she was either in jail or with different boyfriends. There were all kinds of violence and abuse in his home. When he was three years old, his mother left him at a bus stop and took off with a boyfriend. For years this young man was in and out of foster homes and detention centers. He slept in abandoned buildings, in the woods, anyplace he could find. He had to steal food in order to survive. How could he ever make anything out of his life? All the odds were against him, and it wasn't his fault. He didn't have a fair shot in life. But in the seventh grade at a small inner-city school, he met a junior high counselor named Cindy. She could tell this young boy was troubled and had no stability, and she took a great interest in him and in getting his education back on track. But this boy was only in her school for several months before he dropped out. Every day for two years Cindy prayed, "God, please send him back to our school." In the ninth grade, he came walking through the doors. Cindy was right there waiting for him.

Nobody had ever been looking for this young man. His home life was so dysfunctional that every morning Cindy would drive forty-five minutes to pick him up and bring him to school. Her motto was, "Correction does much, but encouragement does more." The following summer he was mowing the lawn of an elderly couple. When they learned his story, they opened their home and took him in. They discovered this young boy had a gift of music, writing, and singing. He started performing at talent shows and community events. Every time, this elderly lady would be in the front row with her Bible in hand, cheering on this young man named Jimmy Wayne. In 2008, his song "Do You Believe Me Now?" hit number one on the country charts. He has toured with Brad Paisley and other music stars. Today he uses his country music platform to raise awareness about foster care and to help other children in the same situation.

As with Jimmy, the odds may be against you. You don't see any way your situation can work out. But God has the right people already lined up. The gifts He has put in you, the dreams, they didn't get canceled because you had bad breaks, because somebody did you wrong. They are still alive. You can still become who God created you to be. It may feel like the fire has been turned up seven times hotter, but don't worry. Your time is coming. God is saying, "The odds are for you. Things are about to change in your favor. That problem that looks permanent, it's only temporary." Now, all through the day, say, "Father, thank You that the odds are for me." If you do this, I believe and declare that, like Jimmy, you're going to go further than you've ever dreamed; like the three Hebrew teenagers, you are going to come out of that fire without the smell of smoke; and, like Lazarus, God is going to make you a living testimony.

CHAPTER FOUR

Move Up to the Next Level

We all have things that are trying to hold us back, whether it's guilt from past mistakes, temptations that we can't seem to overcome, or a dysfunction that's been passed down to us. It's easy to learn to accept it and think that's who we are, but God didn't create you to go through life weighed down by addictions, dysfunction, guilt, or the past. He created you to be free. When Jesus hung on the cross, before He took His final breath, He said, "It is finished." He wasn't just talking about His life and how He had finished His purpose. He was putting an end to all the negative things that could keep us from our destiny. He was saying, in effect, "The guilt is finished. The depression is finished. The low self-esteem is finished. The mediocrity is finished. It is all finished."

Instead of accepting the addiction and thinking, *This is the way it's always going to be. Everybody in my family has it*, you need to announce to that addiction, "It is finished. You don't control me. You can't keep me from my destiny. The price has been paid. I am free. I am clean. I am whole." As long as you accept the addiction, you're allowing it to stay. But when you tell the addiction, tell the past mistakes, tell the poverty, "It is finished. This is not who I am. I am blessed. I am prosperous. I am victorious," in the unseen realm, strongholds are broken, chains are loosed, and favor is released.

Are there things you're living with to which you need to say, "It is finished"? Are you going around feeling guilty, down on yourself because of past mistakes, not expecting anything good? You need to announce to that guilt, "It is finished. I'm done beating myself up, living condemned. God's mercy is bigger than my mistakes. I am redeemed. I am restored. I am forgiven, and I am excited about my future." Are you living with a sense of shame, feeling inferior because of how somebody treated you? Perhaps they did you wrong and walked away, and now the accuser whispers, "It's because you're not good enough. You're not attractive enough. You don't deserve to be loved." Announce to that shame, "It is finished. I'm not inferior or unworthy. I know who I am. I am a child of the Most High God. I'm wearing a crown of favor. I have royal blood flowing through my veins."

No matter what someone did or didn't do to you, it does not change who you are. You may have had bad breaks and gone through unfair situations, but don't have a victim mentality; have a victor mentality. God says He will pay you back double for the unfair things that have happened. That person who did you wrong and thought they were hurting you—the truth is, they were helping you. They qualified you for double. They thought they were setting you back, but in reality they were setting you up. Now, do your part and say to the self-pity, "It is finished. I'm not living discour-

> *No matter what someone did or didn't do to you, it does not change who you are.*

aged, dwelling on my disappointments, and reliving my hurts. I'm letting go of the old, and I'm moving up to the next level that God has in store for me. Father, thank You that double is coming my way."

"Do You Want to Get Well?"

We all can find a reason to live negatively, thinking we're at a disadvantage. You might have been overlooked by your boss or had somebody walk out of a relationship with you. I'm asking you to get rid of the excuses. It's time to say, "It is finished. I'm done thinking about what I didn't get, what didn't work out, who hurt me." You have to tell the past, tell the self-pity, tell the discouragement, "It is finished." As long as you justify your condition, you're giving it permission to stay.

In John 5, Jesus met a disabled man who was lying by the pool of Bethesda in Jerusalem and had been an invalid for thirty-eight years. Surrounding this pool there were five porches that were filled with sick people who were waiting for those certain times when an angel would stir the waters and the first person to get in would be healed. When Jesus saw the man lying there, He asked him, "Do you want to get well?" It seemed as though the answer was obvious, because everyone at the pool was there to be healed. Nevertheless, the Scripture states that Jesus asked him, "Do you want to get well?" In other words, there was nothing in this man's actions or his behavior or his attitude that said he wanted to get well, nothing that said, "I'm expecting things to change." He had his bed there by the porch, and I can imagine that he had his whole area set up around it—a table, a lamp, books, pictures. Over the course of thirty-eight years, he had gotten comfortable in his dysfunction. He thought, *This is my lot in life. It's never going to get better.* He was surrounded by other people who were sick, who were blind, who were afflicted. He gravitated to people who were like him. Everyone there was needy. Everyone there was complaining. Everyone there was discouraged.

You need to be careful about whom you surround yourself with, especially in difficult times. You may have an illness, but don't go find other sick people to hang around. Misery loves company. If you struggle with an addiction, don't hang out with people who are addicted. That's going to cause you to get stuck. If you're depressed, don't go find five depressed friends so you all can be depressed together. Find people who have what you want. If you're struggling

> *You need to be careful about whom you surround yourself with, especially in difficult times.*

in your finances, get around blessed people, generous people, people who are well off. If you tend to be negative and critical, don't stay around people who are like that. Find people who are happy, positive, and grateful. There should be something about you that says, "I want to get well. I want to be blessed. I want to go to the next level."

When Jesus asked this man if he wanted to get well, instead of saying, "Yes, that's what I'm believing for, that's my dream," he said, "Sir, I don't have anybody to help me get in the water. When the water is stirred up, somebody always beats me in." He was justifying his condition. He was saying, "I'm this way because I'm at a disadvantage. Nobody will help me." As long as you're making excuses for where you are, you're going to get stuck. "I'm this way, Joel, because I had a bad childhood. I'm bitter because a business partner cheated me. I'm negative because I have this illness." I'm asking you to get rid of the excuses. Nothing that's happened to you has to keep you from your destiny. If it were going to stop your purpose, God wouldn't allow it. You may not understand it, it may not be fair, but if you will take the hand you've been dealt and make the most of it, God will get you to where you're supposed to be. No person, no bad break, no addiction, and no sickness can stop you. God has the final say. Tell the self-pity, "It is finished." Tell the excuses, "It is finished." This is a new day. God is about to do a new thing.

Jesus said to the disabled man, "Get up! Pick up your bed and walk." Instantly the man was healed. He stood up, picked up his bed, and was able to walk out of there. What you think is permanent, what looks as though it's never going to change—that addiction you've had for years, the illness, the situation in your finances—you don't see a way, but God has a way. Right now, He's fighting your battles. Things are changing in your favor. It may look permanent, but God is saying, "It's only temporary. I'm about to turn it around." Breakthroughs are headed your way. Start looking for new beginnings, for healing, for freedom.

What's interesting is that this disabled man didn't have a lot of faith. He didn't say, "Yes, I believe I can get well." He made excuses, yet God in His mercy healed him. Imagine how God feels when He sees you shaking off the self-pity, shaking off the excuses, and saying, "Lord, I believe You can turn my child around. I believe You'll take me to the next level. I believe You'll free me from this addiction." When you believe, God will make things happen that you couldn't make happen. Tell the excuses, tell the doubt, tell the negative thoughts, "It is finished." It's time to put a stop to the things that are trying to hold you back.

Be the Difference Maker

In the first chapter, I described how my father grew up in a very poor family of cotton farmers who lost everything during the Great Depression. He went to school with holes in his pants and holes in his shoes. He started life at a disadvantage, with no money, very little education, and no future to speak of. The odds were all against him. He had a good excuse to settle where he was and accept a life of mediocrity. But at the age of seventeen, when he gave his life to Christ, he could feel seeds of greatness rising up, seeds of increase, seeds of abundance. On the outside, everything said, "You're poor. You're at a disadvantage. You're limited. You don't have a future." But down in his spirit, he could hear God whispering, "This is not who you are. You can do better than this. You can set a new standard. You were made for more."

When he told his parents he was going to leave the farm and become a minister, they thought he had lost his mind. They

> *You can set a new standard. You were made for more.*

said, "John, you better stay here on the farm with us. All you know how to do is pick cotton." They meant well, but sometimes well-meaning people will try to talk you out of your destiny. If my father had stayed in that limited environment, he would never have seen the fullness of what God had in store.

You have to separate yourself from people who see you only for who you used to be and not for who you're about to become. Some people who knew you back then will try to keep you in the same box that you grew up in. They'll try to put limitations on you: "You can't accomplish that dream. You're not that talented. You'd better play it safe."

In the Scripture, this is what happened with David. His family didn't see him as a giant killer or as a king. They discounted him. David's father, Jesse, didn't even bother to bring him in from the shepherds' field when the prophet Samuel was choosing one of his eight sons as the next king of Israel. Jesse thought, *Ah, it's just David. He's so small and so young. He doesn't*

> *You need to distance yourself from people who are always trying to put limitations on you and talk you out of what God has put in your heart.*

have the experience. But people don't determine your destiny. What they say about you and how they try to make you feel cannot stop what God has ordained for your life. You need to distance yourself from people who are always trying to put limitations on you and talk you out of what God has put in your heart. Sometimes that includes the people who have known you the longest, because they can see you only one way.

Jesus' own brothers did not believe in Him until after He rose from the dead. He was performing miracle after miracle, but they didn't see Him as the Messiah. They only saw Him as their brother and thought, *Oh, it's just Jesus. There's nothing special about Him. We grew up with Him.* Even when Jesus began to gain popularity, the Scripture tells us that His brothers scoffed at Him and made fun of Him. "Yeah, right. You're the Messiah!" They tried to discount Him and talk Him out of His destiny. Jesus let it go in one ear and out the other.

My father could have stayed in that limited environment and accepted a life of poverty and lack. He could have lived with a scarcity mind-set, but he did what I'm asking you to do. He rose up and said, "It is finished. This may be where I am, but this is not who I am." At seventeen years of age, he took a step of faith, left the farm, and started ministering wherever he found the opportunity. God began to promote him and open doors, and eventually he and my mom founded Lakewood, where he pastored for forty years. He went on to live a blessed, abundant life. My point is that my father broke the curse of poverty in our family. Now my siblings and I, and all our families and children, are living at a higher level because one man didn't settle for the status quo. One man didn't say, "I'm at a disadvantage. I've had bad breaks. This is as good as it gets." Instead, he said, "It is finished. I'm a difference maker. I can set a new standard."

You can be the difference maker for your family. You can put an end to negative things that have been passed down. What you're dealing with may not have started with you, but it can stop with you. You need to say to the poverty, say to the lack, "It is finished. I will lend and not borrow." Say to the addiction, the depression, the dysfunction, "It is finished." God wants

> *Just because negative things have been passed down to you doesn't mean they're supposed to continue with you.*

you to set a new standard. You have seeds of greatness. You are full of talent, ideas, and potential. You're not limited by where you came from. Just because negative things have been passed down to you doesn't mean they're supposed to continue with you. You're the one who can break the curse, break the poverty, break the depression, break the dysfunction.

You can take your family to the new level. Don't talk yourself out of it. Don't let circumstances discourage you. The odds may be against you, but the Most High God is for you. He is breathing in your direction right now. He's going to open doors that no man can shut, bring talent out of you that you hadn't known you had, and He'll cause the right people to be good to you. Opportunities are going to track you down—good breaks, freedom, and increase. You're stepping into the next level. Bondages that have held you and your family back are being broken. Now, do your part and have a new mind-set—an abundant mentality, a free mentality, a healthy mentality, a victorious mentality. I wouldn't be where I am if my father had kept that poverty mind-set, that scarcity mentality, thinking, *I'm at a disadvantage. I've had bad breaks.*

Where You Come from Is Not Who You Are

We all could come up with excuses to settle where we are. I'm asking you to get rid of the excuses. It's time to announce to anything that's holding you back, "It is finished. This is a new day. I'm drawing the line in the sand. As for me and my house, we will serve the Lord. We will live free from addictions. We will lend and not borrow, and we will be generous and help others. We will accomplish our dreams and become everything we were created to be."

I have a friend who's very successful today. His father was a police officer, and he was raised in a middle-class home. When he was eleven years old, his father told him to get in the car and said they were going to take a drive together. They drove for several hours to another state, and his father never told him where he was taking him. Finally they came to a very run-down neighborhood, with trash lying around everywhere and none of the buildings kept up. My young friend's eyes were wide open; he'd never seen anything like it. They pulled into a makeshift dirt driveway of a house that was completely dilapidated. There was no front door, the windows were broken out, and it looked like it was vacant. He followed his father into the house, and he was shocked to find an old man in the front room sitting on a stool. The man was shirtless, hadn't shaved, and looked like he was homeless. His father looked at this man and said, "Dad, I brought my son to see you." My friend couldn't believe that this man could be his grandfather. He'd never even seen a photo of his grandfather before and had never heard his father talk about him. The grandfather wouldn't look up. He didn't want anything to do with his son or his grandson. My friend's father put some money on the counter and said, "Dad, I love you. I just wanted to say hi." Then he turned around, and the two of them walked out of the shack. My friend said, "Dad, that was the most afraid I've been in my whole life. I never want to come back to this place." His father said, "Son, that's why I brought you here—to show you this is where we come from, but this is not who we are."

You might have been raised in a limited environment. Perhaps your family members were good people, but they didn't have any vision for a better future and they settled for mediocrity. As it was with my friend,

> *Where you start is not important. Where you finish is what matters.*

you can set a new standard. Where you start is not important. Where you finish is what matters. God is going to use you not just to break a generational curse, but to start a generational blessing. Where you come from is not who you are. You are blessed, you are free, you are talented, and you are a child of the Most High God.

In the Scripture, Abraham was living in a limited environment. God told him to leave his country, to leave his extended family behind, and go to a land that He would show him. God was saying, "Abraham, you have to leave what's familiar, leave what you grew up with." I'm not suggesting that you abandon your family, but I am saying to leave behind the negative mind-sets you were raised with. Leave a scarcity mentality. Leave the limitations that people have put on you. You have to make room for God to increase you. Sometimes our environment is too small. It's like the oak tree seed that I mentioned previously. If you plant it and leave it in a five-gallon pot, that oak tree will never become what it was created to be. It's not because there's something wrong with the tree. It's because of the environment that it's in.

In the same way, there's nothing wrong with you. You have seeds of greatness in you. The Most High God breathed His life into you. Now make sure your pot is not too small. Make sure your environment is not holding you back. You need to be around people who inspire you, people who have gone further, people who are making a difference, not just people who are settling for the status quo. The prophet Isaiah says, "Enlarge the place of your tent. Stretch forth your curtains. Lengthen your cords. Strengthen your stakes. Make room for God to do a new thing." Tell that limited mind-set, "It is finished. I'm dreaming big dreams. I'm praying bold prayers. I'm expecting to go further than how I was raised."

When You Don't Understand

After my father went to be with the Lord in 1999, many people asked me if I thought we could keep the church going. I never answered them arrogantly, but I told them, "I don't think we can just keep it going. I believe we can go further." It's because God is a progressive God. He wants every generation to increase. Have a bigger vision. Don't settle for what your parents had, what your relatives accomplished. You were made for more. You can be the one to set the new standard.

It's easy to talk ourselves out of our dreams and live discouraged because of disappointments and things we don't understand. We worked hard, but we didn't get the promotion. We prayed, but our loved one didn't make it. We did our best, but the relationship didn't work out. Life is not always fair. I can't explain why things happen as they do, but I can tell you that God says He will take what was meant for your harm and use it to your advantage. He says He will pay you back double for the unfair things that happened. He says He will give you beauty for the ashes, but I've learned you have to let go of the ashes before you receive the beauty. You can't hold on to the old and expect to receive the new. The past is over and done. That's why it's called the past. Quit dwelling on it, quit reliving it. You're not

> *You can't hold on to the old and expect to receive the new.*

going to understand everything that happens, but God has a purpose for it. He knows how to bring good out of it. So keep moving forward.

This is what David did. He had a newborn baby who became very sick. Night and day David prayed and fasted for this baby. He wouldn't eat and wouldn't talk with anyone else. He spent all his time on his knees, asking God to heal his child. On the seventh day, the little baby died. David's attendants didn't know how he would handle the news, but when they told him, David got up off the ground, took a shower, put on new clothes, and went to the temple and began to worship God. When he finished, he went and had dinner with his men. They were so amazed, and they asked him, "David, why are you acting this way? When the child was living, you wept and refused to eat, but now that he has died, you've stopped your mourning and you're acting as though everything's okay." David said, "When the child was alive, I asked God to let him live. But now that he has died, I cannot bring him back, but one day I will go to be with him." David did everything he could. He prayed, he fasted, and he believed, but it didn't work out his way. He could have lived bitter, with a chip on his shoulder, but David understood this principle. He said to the past, "It is finished. I don't understand it, but I'm moving forward."

We all have things in life that we don't understand. It's easy to live negatively, with a chip on our shoulder. But if we're going to receive the double, if we're going to see the beauty for ashes, we have to do as David did and say to the past, say to the things you don't understand, "It is finished. I'm not going to dwell on what didn't work out. I'm not going to try to figure out why. I'm going to let it go and keep moving up to the next level." The past doesn't have to stop you. That bad break, that loss, that disappointment—God is in control of your life. You wouldn't be alive unless He had something amazing in front of you. You haven't had too many bad breaks, you haven't made too many mistakes. You're on the verge

Get ready for the new things God is about to do.

of receiving double. You're on the verge of beauty for ashes. Now, do your part and put on a new attitude, wash your face, and get ready for the new things God is about to do.

Let me declare this over you: The past, the hurts, the regrets—it is finished. The poverty, the lack, the limited mind-sets—it is finished. The addictions, the depression, the dysfunction, the guilt, the shame, the self-pity—it is finished. This is a new day. Things that have held you back are being broken right now. You're going to step into a new level of freedom. You're going to break generational curses and start generational blessings. You're about to see beauty for ashes, healing, promotion, and breakthroughs. It's headed your way!

CHAPTER FIVE

Recognize Your Value

Too often we base our value on how someone is treating us, how successful we are, how perfect a life we've lived. The problem is that all those things can change. If you're trying to get your value from how people treat you, then if they hurt or disappoint you, you're going to feel devalued. If you're basing your value upon your achievements—how much money you make, what type of car you drive, the title behind your name—then if something happens and you don't have that position or your business goes down, your sense of value will go down.

Some people don't feel good about themselves because they've made mistakes in life. They're not where they thought they would be. Now they're living with insecurities, feeling inferior. They're basing their value on their performance, but here's the key: Your value should be based solely on the fact that you are a child of the Most High God. The Creator of the universe breathed His life into you. How someone treats you doesn't change your value. What they say about you or do to you doesn't lessen who you are. Mistakes you've made don't decrease your value. That's what you did; that's not who you are. You can buy a bigger house, drive a more luxurious car, and get the big promotion you've worked so hard for, but that doesn't make you more valuable. That increases your net worth, not your self-worth. You were just as valuable when you had the small apartment and no title behind your name. That position may give you more influence, but not more value. If you're a stay-at-home mom raising your children, you might not have the influence of a CEO, but you have the same value.

Value is not based on what you do, what your income is, or who you know. Those are all superficial. Those things can change. Next level thinking says that your value comes from your Creator. God breathed His life into you. You have the DNA of

Almighty God. You have royalty in your blood, but the enemy works overtime trying to devalue you. He'd love for you to go through life letting what people say about you make you feel inferior, comparing your life to other people's lives and thinking you'll feel good about yourself as soon as you catch up to them. Perhaps when you live in that more affluent neighborhood, when you perform perfectly, when you break the addiction, then you'll feel valuable.

But nothing you ever do, nothing you ever achieve, and nothing you ever overcome will make you any more valuable. You are valuable right now. God calls you a masterpiece. You are one of a kind. You didn't come off an assembly line. You weren't mass-produced. God made you unique. There will never be

> *Nothing you ever do, nothing you ever achieve, and nothing you ever overcome will make you any more valuable.*

another you. Put your shoulders back. Start carrying yourself with confidence. You have been fearfully and wonderfully made.

You Have Nothing to Prove

In Luke 4, Jesus was led by the Spirit into the wilderness, where He was tempted by the enemy three
times. He'd been out there for forty days and hadn't
eaten anything. The enemy said to Jesus, "If You are
the Son of God, tell this stone to become bread."
He was trying to get Jesus to base His value on His
performance. The enemy was saying, "If You turn
this stone into bread, You can prove You're the Son
of God, and then You can feel good about Yourself.
You performed a miracle." Jesus refused to do it. He
said, "Man doesn't live by bread alone." He was saying, in effect, "I don't have to do anything to prove
Who I am. I don't have to perform to feel good
about Myself. I know Who I am."

The enemy couldn't deceive Jesus into basing His
value upon His performance, so in the second temptation he tried to go with a possession-based value. He
took Jesus to a high place and showed Him all the
kingdoms of the world in a moment of time. The
enemy said, "You can have it all, if You'll just bow
down and worship me." Jesus answered him, "No,
thanks. I don't need possessions to prove My worth

and value. I don't have to have what you think is important to feel good about Who I am."

Possession-based value didn't work with Jesus, nor did performance-based value, so the enemy tried one final temptation: a popularity-based value. He took Jesus to the highest point of the temple. It was very crowded below with all kinds of people. He said, "If You are the Son of God, jump off this building. You said Your angels would protect You from any harm." He was trying to get Jesus to show off. Everybody in the temple area would see Him floating to the ground and be amazed. He'd gain instant popularity. Jesus answered the enemy again, "I don't need possessions. I don't need performance. I don't need popularity to feel valuable. I know Who I am. I'm the Son of the living God."

> *"I don't need possessions. I don't need performance. I don't need popularity to feel valuable. I know Who I am."*

The enemy tried to deceive Jesus into proving Who He was. Many people live in a proving mode. They can't feel good about themselves unless they prove to people that they are important, prove to their coworkers that they are talented, and prove to their critics that they really are okay. There is a constant struggle going on in their lives. They are always having to outdo, outperform, outdrive, and outdress somebody else. It's very freeing when you realize you don't have to prove anything to anyone. You don't have to impress people. It takes the pressure off, because it takes a lot of energy to constantly compete, to prove, to impress. If you live in a proving mode, it's as though you're running on a treadmill that never stops. As soon as you prove to one person that you're okay, you'll see somebody else you need to impress. It's a never-ending cycle. You have to get off that treadmill. You're working hard but going nowhere. You don't have to prove anything to anyone.

Be Secure in Who You Are

Today there's so much emphasis on name brands. We're wearing so-and-so designer shoes and so-and-so sunglasses, carrying a so-and-so purse, driving a so-and-so car, and talking on a so-and-so phone. If you're *really* cool, you have on so-and-so underwear. Sometimes we have so many other names on us that we don't know our own name. We're counting on all the name brands, all the outside labels, to make us feel important. Can I tell you that your name is more important than all those names combined? No disrespect to them, but the difference between you and a name brand is that God breathed His life into you. You're a son, you're a daughter, of the Most High God. There's nothing wrong with owning it, driving it, or wearing it, but don't let that be the reason that you feel good about who you are, because what's hot today, what's the latest and greatest, in a few years will be outdated.

If you live with possession-based values, you have to run from name to name, position to position, and friend to friend. That's going to wear you out. Why don't you relax? You can't get any more valuable than you already are at this very moment. You can buy more clothes, add titles to your résumé, and get more friends, but that doesn't change your value.

> *Whether you're wearing Gucci or Goodwill, whether it's Calvin Klein or Fruit of the Loom, your value never changes.*

Whether you're wearing Gucci or Goodwill, whether it's Calvin Klein or Fruit of the Loom, your value never changes.

I went to the sporting goods store the other day to buy some new T-shirts to work out in, and there were probably ten racks of T-shirts alone. Practically every shirt had a manufacturer's name on the front in big bold letters. I thought to myself, *You want me to buy your T-shirt and then walk around as a billboard for you. No offense, but I don't want to wear your name. I like my own name.* Do you need somebody else's name to make you feel good about yourself? Are you trying to prove your worth, your value, by who you know, what you wear, or what you drive? Or can you say, as Jesus did, "I don't have to have popularity, possessions, or performance to feel good about myself. I am secure in who I am"?

Don't Give Away Your Identity

When Jesus was riding into Jerusalem on a young donkey to celebrate the Passover feast, a large crowd of people laid down palm branches as He passed by. They celebrated His arrival, shouting, "Hosanna! Blessed is He who comes in the name of the Lord!" From the youngest to the oldest, they waved and cheered. They were so excited to see Him. He received a hero's welcome. But a few days later, those same people, instead of shouting, "Hosanna!" were shouting, "Crucify Him! We don't want Him here!" When Jesus went to trial and needed His closest friends to support Him, most of His disciples, the ones He had poured His life into, weren't anywhere around. When He asked them to stay up and pray, they were too tired. They fell asleep.

If you base your value on people's support, how much they approve you and encourage you, then if for some reason they stop doing that, you'll feel devalued. As long as they're telling you, "You're great," you'll feel great. The problem is, if they change their minds and stop telling you that, you're not going to feel great. You can't base your value on what people give or don't give you. People are often unreliable. One day, they'll say, "You're beautiful," and the next, "I don't care for you." "Hosanna!" on Palm Sunday, and "Crucify Him!" on Good Friday.

If you don't know who you are without other people, then if they leave, you'll be lost. They'll take you with them, because your identity was caught up in who they made you to be. Then you'll have to try to find somebody else to tell you who you are. But you don't need other people to tell you who you are. People will let you

> *If you don't know who you are without other people, then if they leave, you'll be lost. They'll take you with them.*

down. People will get jealous. People have their own issues. Let your heavenly Father tell you who you are. Get your value, your self-worth, your approval from Him. He says you're a masterpiece. He says you're one of a kind, a prized possession.

Somebody may have told you the opposite. "You're not talented." "You're not attractive." "You don't have a good personality." Let that go in one ear and out the other. They don't determine your value. What they say or do to you doesn't make you any less a masterpiece. Quit letting how people treat you make you feel inferior. They don't control your destiny. They didn't breathe life into you. They didn't call you. They didn't anoint you. They didn't approve you. Your value came from your Creator, from the God Who spoke worlds into existence. The good news is they can't change your value, and you can't change it either. God put it in you before you showed up. You don't need their approval. You don't need their encouragement. They don't have to validate you. It's good when they do; it feels good.

But if you're depending on it to make you feel secure, then if they don't do it, you're going to feel inferior. Don't give away your power. Don't put your identity, your value, into somebody else's hands.

You Are a Masterpiece

Even good people who love you very much can't give you everything you need. They cannot keep you approved, validated, and feeling secure. You have to go to your heavenly Father. Sometimes we're putting pressure on people to keep us fixed, to keep us feeling validated. Let them off the hook. They're not your Savior. You already have a Savior. He's on the throne. Go to Him and not to people. The problem with trying to get this from other people is they have their own issues. Other people are dealing with insecurities, fears, hurts, wounds, prejudices, and dysfunctions. They don't know any better. That's normal to them. Messed-up people can mess you up. That's not profound, but it's true. If you base your value on what they're giving you, you can end up dysfunctional.

I talked with a lady recently who had a very bad

childhood that was filled with neglect and abuse. She had just gone through her second divorce, with her ex-husband telling her over and over that she didn't deserve to be loved. I could tell she had come to believe it because she was down on herself, with no expression on her face. I told her what I'm telling you: "Don't let messed-up people ruin the rest of your life." If somebody hurts you, there's a tendency to internalize it and think, *There is something wrong with me. If I were more attractive, he wouldn't have left. If I were smarter, I wouldn't have had a bad childhood.* No, it has nothing to do with you. How they are treating you flows from their own hurts, their own wounds. Hurting people end up hurting other people. Don't let what they say about you define who you are. Don't let what you didn't get from them make you feel as though you're to blame. They said you don't deserve to be loved. That's a lie. They said you're not attractive. Another lie. But if you base your value on these lies, you won't have any self-worth. Studies have shown that children who went through neglect and abuse in their childhood very often take the blame on themselves. They think there's something wrong with them. This lady did the same thing well into her adulthood.

She didn't think she deserved to be loved. That's the enemy trying to steal your sense of value. If somebody did you wrong, rather than internalize it, as she did,

> *Hurting people end up hurting other people.*

have you ever thought that they hurt you because they were messed up? Maybe they felt so badly about themselves, so unlovable, that they tried to project it onto you.

I know a young man who never felt like he fit in. Growing up, there was very little love in his home. He never felt approved or celebrated. It was as though he was a burden. When he was in his early teens, he found out that his parents had always wanted a girl. They had been disappointed when he was born. Now he's in his twenties, walking around with his head down and feeling insecure and unworthy. I told him, "Your parents may have wanted a girl, but the Creator of the universe wanted a boy. God doesn't make mistakes. You're not an accident. He handpicked you. He chose you before you could choose Him. Your parents might not have known any better, but don't let their lack of approval keep you from your destiny. You didn't come *from* your mother. You came

through your mother. You came from Almighty God."
I began to tell him how he was a masterpiece, called,
chosen, equipped, one of a kind, with seeds of greatness. Nobody had ever spoken faith over his life. He
lifted his head and put his shoulders back. I could
see a smile starting to form.

When you base your value on what other people
say or do to you, that's going to push you down. But
when you base it on what God says about you, it's
going to lift you up to the next level. You're going
to have a smile on your face, a spring in your step.
You're not going to be put off by what you didn't get
or by who's not supporting you. As it was with this
young man, maybe nobody ever told you what God
says about you. God says you're amazing. He says
He's proud of you. He says you're the apple of His
eye. People may not be celebrating you, but you need
to know that God celebrates you. I've heard it said
that if God had a refrigerator, your picture would
be on it. If He had a computer, your photo would be on
the screen saver. The Scripture says that God has
your name engraved on the palms of His hands. He's
always thinking about you.

There's Only One Whose Approval Really Matters

You may feel as though you never received the approval from your parents or your family. Even now, they don't celebrate you. They don't affirm you. But the truth is, it's not about you. It's about their own issues, their own insecurities. Don't spend your life trying to get something from them that they cannot give. I know people who work eighty hours a week trying to prove to their parents that they're successful, trying to prove to their family that they're good enough. You have to let it go or you'll be frustrated. Turn to your heavenly Father. Receive your approval from Him. He's smiling down on you. He loves you just the way He made you. You don't have to have other people's approval to be happy. God approves you. He's the only One Who really matters.

In the Scripture, as I mentioned in Chapter Four, David didn't have his father's approval or the approval of his seven

> *Sometimes the people closest to you can't see the greatness in you.*

brothers. When the prophet Samuel came to their

home in Bethlehem to anoint one of Jesse's sons to be the next king, David was the only son whom his father left out as a candidate. For some reason Jesse saw David as being inferior to his other sons. Perhaps he thought David was not as talented as the others, not as tall and strong and experienced. Sometimes the people closest to you can't see the greatness in you. Jesse didn't see a king in David. He didn't see a giant killer or a strategic leader. He saw a young man who had little to offer. Jesse dismissed him, didn't pay much attention to him, and later David's oldest brother, Eliab, treated David in a similar manner when David was about to fight Goliath. The people who should have supported him the most tried to make him feel inferior.

Your own family may discount you. The people closest to you may not acknowledge your gifts and may leave you out, but don't take it personally. Just keep being your best, receiving your approval from your heavenly Father. David was left out, and it wasn't fair. But when Samuel looked at Jesse's other seven sons, he said, "The Lord has not chosen any of these, Jesse. Do you have any more sons?" People may leave you out, but God doesn't leave you out. If David had

had to have his family's approval, he would never have taken the throne.

Quit trying to make people be for you who are never going to be for you. Quit feeling inferior because somebody close to you is not celebrating you. If you needed their approval, you would get it. If you're not getting it, that means you don't need it to become who you were created to be. Yes, it may be hurtful, but it is not going to keep you from your destiny. Sometimes it's God teaching us to go to Him and not to people. We rely too much on what people think about us, on who seems to believe in us, and think too much about why they are not supporting us. David's brothers made fun of him. His father discounted him. He was stuck out in the shepherds' fields. But instead of complaining and feeling inferior, he turned to God. David is the one who wrote in Psalm 27: "If my mother and father forsake me, God will adopt me as His own child."

Your Value Comes from Your Maker

Many of us had great parents who did their best, but we all have some people in our lives who are not

> *We all have some people in our lives who are not giving us their approval.*

giving us their approval. They don't acknowledge our gifts. They don't see what we have to offer.

Don't live frustrated, thinking there is something wrong with you, trying to prove to them who you are, trying to convince them to affirm you. Let it go. There's nothing wrong with you. If you had to have their approval, they would give it. Since you don't, shake it off. Keep your head held high, knowing that your heavenly Father has approved you, accepted you, and anointed you. Your value doesn't come from people. It comes from your Creator.

A while back I was out of town, at one of our events, and a man came up and handed me a small box and said that he so appreciated our ministry that he wanted to give it as a gift. I opened it, and there was a beautiful watch. It wasn't super fancy, but it was attractive and sporty, and, of course, I thanked him and was very grateful. I brought it back and put it in my desk drawer for safekeeping until I could turn it over to the person who handles ministry gifts. A couple of months later, I opened the drawer to get something out, and there was the watch. I had forgotten about it. I looked it over again and thought it probably cost a couple hundred dollars, then I decided to google it. When I did, I nearly passed out. The exact watch came up and was worth over $10,000! It came from a very famous, prestigious watchmaker. Because of the manufacturer, this watch was extremely valuable. You could put it side by side with a lot of other watches I've seen that cost several hundred dollars, and you wouldn't see much difference. It looked average, ordinary. But the other manufacturers had copied it. Their watches are knockoffs. On the surface, this watch seemed the same, but what gave it a higher value was who made it.

Sometimes we don't realize who we are. You may feel average, ordinary, as though nothing stands out, but because of your Maker, there's something about you that makes you extremely valuable. You're not a copy. You're not a knockoff. You're an original. The Creator of the universe is your manufacturer. You can't get any more prestigious than that. But if you don't know who you are, like I didn't know the watch's maker, you'll discount yourself, thinking, *Oh, man, I'm just ordinary. I have nothing much to offer. There's nothing special about me.* You need to google your manufacturer. You have the fingerprints of God all over you. Psalm 139 says, "God, I praise You because You have made me in an amazing way. What You have done is wonderful."

If you're going to recognize your value, you have to see yourself as amazing, as wonderful. It's not because of who you are, but because of Who made you. Life will try to make you feel as though you're anything but amazing. Disappointments, betrayals, and rejection will try to steal your sense of value. But all through the day, despite what your thoughts are telling you, despite who left you out or said something negative about you, you need to remind yourself, "I am amazing. I am a masterpiece. I have been wonderfully made." Don't discount what God has created. Don't go around feeling ordinary, when in fact you're extraordinary. People may try to make you feel average, as David's father and brothers did to him. They'll tell you that you don't have much to offer.

> *If you're going to recognize your value, you have to see yourself as amazing, as wonderful.*

Are you going to believe what people say about you or believe what God says about you and move up to the next level? God says, "You're amazing!"

Have you ever said that to yourself? It has to start on the inside.

I read that the football jersey Tom Brady wore during Super Bowl LI is worth $500,000. I can go online and buy that same jersey for $49. What's the difference? Who it belongs to. Same jersey, same size, same color, but only one belongs to Tom Brady. That makes it extremely valuable. The Scripture says you belong to God. You may feel average and think you look ordinary and that there's nothing special about you. But because of Who you belong to, that makes you extremely valuable. My challenge is, don't let people discount you. Don't let your own thoughts push you down. Put your shoulders back. You belong to God. You don't have to prove anything. You don't have to try to impress people. Just be who you are. Be amazing. If you do this, I believe and declare every chain that's held you back is being broken. You're going to live free, confidently, and securely, knowing you are valuable. You will become the masterpiece that God created you to be.

CHAPTER SIX

Live with the Boldness of a Son

We all have been through disappointments and had unfair situations. Because of negative things in the past or even mistakes we've made, it's easy to forget who we really are. Too often, we've developed a slave mentality. We think we're at a disadvantage, so we don't pursue our dreams, we don't believe for good breaks, and we don't pray bold prayers. We live as though we're a slave to an addiction, a slave to depression, a slave to mediocrity, a slave to others' approval. But as long as we have a slave mentality, it will limit our life. The Scripture says, "Beloved, now are you the sons of God." You may have a lot coming against you, but you are not a slave, you are a son. Sons think differently than slaves. You may struggle with an addiction, but a son says, "I have a right to be free." There may be obstacles in your path, but a son knows the forces for him are greater than the forces against him.

The Israelites had been in slavery in Egypt for four hundred years. They were mistreated and taken advantage of. God saw the injustice and sent plagues on the Pharaoh and his people until Pharaoh finally gave in and decided to let them go. When the Israelites headed out toward the Promised Land, I'm sure they were excited that their dream of freedom had finally come true—until Pharaoh changed his mind and came chasing after them. He took six hundred of his fastest chariots, his strongest warriors, and his army, and he was quickly approaching as the Israelites came to a dead end at the Red Sea. They had nowhere to go. Pharaoh was saying, in effect, "You're my slaves. I own you, and I'm taking you back." God was saying, "You're my sons and daughters. I've redeemed you. I'm taking you forward into freedom." I can imagine that this debate was playing back and forth in the minds of the Israelites. They were trying to choose whom they were going to believe: "You're a son" or "You're a slave."

That same debate is taking place about you. One voice is saying, "You're a slave. You'll never get well.

You'll always struggle in your finances. You'll always be addicted." But God is saying, "You're a son. I've equipped you, empowered you, and anointed you." Now, you get to choose which way you go. If you believe the lie that you're a slave, that you've reached your limits, it will keep you from your purpose. You need to rise up and say, "I'm no longer a slave, I'm a son. I'm not a slave to my past. I'm not a slave to the people who hurt me. I'm not a slave to addiction, to poverty, to lack, or to depression. I'm a child of the Most High God."

When you know you're a son, you not only think differently, but you talk differently. Instead of saying, "I'll never break this addiction," you say, "I am free. I am whole." Instead of complaining, "I never get good breaks," you declare, "Blessings are chasing me down. Favor surrounds me. Goodness and mercy are following me." Stop thinking like a slave and start thinking like a son. Stop thinking about what you were, what you've been through, and the mistakes you've made. Rather, start thinking about who you are—you are free, you are blessed, you are a masterpiece, you are victorious.

> *Stop thinking like a slave and start thinking like a son.*

You Are Not a Slave to Your Past

Pharaoh and his chariots came chasing after the Israelites. In other words, the past came chasing after them, reminding them of what they had been through, what didn't work out. The past will always come chasing after you. The mistakes you've made, the disappointments, the failures, and the hurts are saying, "You're not a son. Look what you've been through. It wasn't fair. You prayed, and it didn't work out." The enemy would love for you to become a slave to your past. He wants you to live feeling guilty, discouraged, and with a chip on your shoulder. Don't fall into that trap. The past doesn't have to hold you back. We all have had negative things happen to us, things we don't understand, but God has beauty for those ashes. He has mercy for our mistakes. He has new beginnings. Nothing that's happened in your past and nothing that you've done have to keep you from the good things God has in store. Don't be a slave to your past. Quit thinking about it, quit reliving the hurts, quit dwelling on the failures, for this is a new day. If you will let go of the old, you'll see the next levels God has in store.

Pharaoh came chasing the Israelites because he thought he owned them. He saw them as his property. You need to tell Pharaoh, tell the enemy, tell the past, tell the addiction, "You don't own me. I was bought with a precious price. I belong to the God Who spoke worlds into existence. I'm not your slave, I'm His son." You have to know who you are and Who you belong to. Fear doesn't have any right to you. It doesn't own you. Poverty doesn't own you. You may have an addiction, but it doesn't own you. Don't see it as your master, as though it is so big and powerful that you'll never be free. No, it's only temporary. It cannot stay. Your body is a temple of the Most High God. You are not a sick person trying to get well. You're a well person fighting off sickness. You are not an addict trying to get free. You're a free person fighting an addiction. You're not a poor person trying to get ahead. You're a prosperous person fighting off poverty. You are not a slave to any negative thing. God created you to be free, healthy, whole, and victorious. And, sure, we all have things come against us, but they're not permanent. It's just a matter of time before it changes in your favor.

> *Fear doesn't have any right to you. It doesn't own you.*

Even if the Israelites escaped from the Pharaoh, in one sense they would always have been runaway slaves. As long as Pharaoh was chasing them, even though they were free, thoughts would tell them, *You're still a slave. You're just a slave that got away. Sooner or later, you'll be caught and taken back.* They would have to live with the threat that Pharaoh would catch up with them sooner or later. But when they reached the dead end at the Red Sea, when they had nowhere else to go, Moses held up his rod and the waters parted. The two million Israelites, all former slaves, went through on dry ground. When Pharaoh and the chariots and his army came chasing, the waters closed up, and they were drowned. God not only freed them from slavery, but He eliminated their oppressor so they wouldn't have to live with the threat that they might be recaptured and taken back to slavery. God didn't want the Israelites to see themselves as just runaway slaves, slaves who had been freed. By taking care of the Pharaoh, by defeating the enemy, He removed that label. They were no longer runaway slaves; now they were simply sons and daughters of the Most High God.

In the same way, God has not only freed us from sin, from guilt, from depression, and from sicknesses, but

He took care of our enemy.
You don't have to live with
the threat that you might be
recaptured. Your oppressor

You're not a runaway slave, you're a son.

has been defeated; the enemy has no power over you.
You're not a runaway slave, you're a son. But here's the
key: after all God has done for us, freeing us from
slavery and defeating our enemy, if you don't see yourself the right way, it will keep you from your destiny.

Get the Slavery Mentality Out

This is what happened to the Israelites. They saw
God free them from slavery through supernatural
plagues in Egypt. They saw God deliver them from
the Pharaoh and his army at the Red Sea. They saw
God provide them with manna to eat and bring water
out of a rock in the wilderness. When they came to
the border of the Promised Land, you would think
they would be full of faith, ready to take the land.
But when the ten spies saw how big the people were,
they told Moses, "We'll never defeat them. They're
too big and too powerful for us. Let's just go back to
Egypt. Let's go back to being slaves." They had been

in slavery for so long and had seen so much injustice that they never quit seeing themselves as slaves. They didn't think they could live at a higher level. Their attitude was, *We're just poor old slaves. We never get any good breaks.* God brought them out of slavery, but slavery never got out of them.

You may have struggled in an area for a long time, but don't have a limited mind-set. You have to give God permission to increase you. It starts in your thinking. You can't see yourself as a slave and enjoy the blessings of a son. If you grew up in lack, not having enough, surrounded by mediocrity, don't let that poverty spirit get in or stay in you. That is not who you are. You're the one to break the curse. You're the one to set a new standard. God is about to let loose resources, promotion, ideas, and opportunities for you. Have a vision for increase. See yourself as a son rising higher. You have seeds of greatness. You are not limited by how you were raised, by your family, by what you didn't get. You're not a slave to lack. You're not a slave to depression. You're not a slave to fear. The oppressor has been defeated. Your days of struggle, your days of sick-

> *Have a vision for increase. See yourself as a son rising higher.*

ness, your days of loneliness are coming to an end. God is about to do a new thing. He's going to break bondages that have held you back. Negative things that have been in your family line for generations are about to turn in your favor.

After four hundred years of slavery in Egypt, after ten generations of oppression and injustice, nothing had changed for the Israelites. They had been born into bondage to slavery year after year and didn't expect anything different. But one day, God said, "Enough is enough," and He supernaturally brought them out. However, although it was good that God freed that first group of two million from slavery, that wasn't God's best. Those people never made it into the Promised Land because they still saw themselves as slaves. But God didn't give up on them. He didn't say, "I'm done with this family." Forty years later, God took their children into the Promised Land, because that next generation had a different mind-set.

I believe that in your family you're going to be the generation that goes into the Promised Land. What your relatives did or didn't do does not have to stop you. You're going to receive houses you didn't build, vineyards you didn't plant, opportunities that chase you down, promotions you didn't deserve, blessings you can't explain, and favor that thrusts you further than you can imagine.

Now, don't talk yourself out of it. "Joel, that's not me. I've reached my limits. My family always struggles." Get rid of that slave mentality and start having an abundant mentality. Even though the oppressor has been taken care of, even though the enemy is defeated, he'll still whisper lies. "You're not supposed to be blessed. You'll always be addicted." What he's really saying is, "You're a slave. Come on, just accept it." Tell him, "No, you have the wrong person. I'm not a slave, I'm a son. I'm blessed, I'm prosperous, and I'm a difference maker. I'm going to set a new standard for my family. We're going into our Promised Land."

Be Bold

A while ago we had a repairman come to our house to fix the air conditioner. He had to come inside the house and go up into the attic. When he came in, he didn't stop by the refrigerator and get something to drink. He didn't sit on my couch and watch some television. He didn't go out my back door and enjoy my backyard.

He went straight to the attic and fixed the problem with the air conditioner. He knew he couldn't come in and make himself at home. He was there as a servant, not as a son. But when our son, Jonathan, comes in, he doesn't ask, "Dad, can I go to the refrigerator and get something to drink? Can I sit here and watch some television?" He doesn't ask for permission; he acts as though he owns the place, and the truth is, he does. He's my son. Everything I have is his. I like the fact that he knows who he is. He's confident in what belongs to him, so he goes boldly to the refrigerator.

The Scripture tells us to come boldly to the throne of grace, not as a servant saying, "God, I know I don't deserve it. I know I'm unworthy." If you want to make God happy, if you want to put a smile on His face, go to Him with boldness, go to Him like you know He's proud of you, like you know you deserve to be there, like you know He wants to be good to you. Ask Him for your dreams. Pray bold prayers. You're not inconveniencing Him. You don't have to earn God's love. You don't have to work for His approval. You don't have to pay God back for your mistakes.

Never once has Jonathan come into our house and said, "Dad, I did wrong today. I don't deserve to eat here. Let me work for you and earn the right to have this meal." If he did that, number one, I'd check his temperature. Number two, as his father, I would be disappointed. I would think, *Doesn't he know he's my son and I always want to be good to him?*

Are you trying to earn God's goodness, trying to be good enough, trying to work hard enough, thinking that then maybe you'll deserve God's blessings? That's a slave mentality. Why don't you start believing that you're a son? You're already in the family. Jesus says, "It is the Father's good pleasure to give you the kingdom." God is longing to be good to you. Are you living like a son, knowing that you have rights, knowing that God is pleased with you? Or are you living like a slave, feeling unworthy, like you don't deserve God's goodness?

> *Why don't you start believing that you're a son?*

You Are a Son Right Now

In the story of the prodigal son in Luke 15, the young man asked his father for his inheritance and left home. He wasted all the money through partying, wild living, and making poor choices. Once he was broke, he was so desperate that he ended up working in a farmer's field, feeding the hogs. He became so hungry that he had to eat the hog food to survive. When he finally came to his senses about what had happened to him, he thought, *The servants at home live better than I do. I'm going to go back to my father's house, and after all the wrongs I've done, after this big mess, I know I can't live at home, but maybe my father will hire me back as one of his servants.* Because of his mistakes, he stopped seeing himself as a son and started seeing himself as a servant. He thought he didn't deserve his father's goodness. He didn't think he had a right to be in the family anymore.

How many of us have disqualified ourselves from God's goodness? We knew at one time we were a son, at one time we knew God was going to help us, favor us, and bless us, but we made poor choices. We got off course. Now we believe the lie that somehow we've gone from a son to a slave, that God won't have anything to do with us.

This young man got his nerve up and headed back home. He was prepared for his father to let him have it, to say, "Don't even think about coming on this property." But as he got closer, he could see his father standing at the end of the driveway. It

looked as though his father was looking for him, as
though he had been waiting for him. All of a sudden,
his father started running toward him. He thought,
*Oh, great, he's going to stop me before I get on the
property. He's going to come out here and yell at me.*
But his father grabbed him and started hugging and
kissing him. The son went into his speech: "Dad,
I don't deserve to be called your son, but maybe
you will hire me back as one of your servants." His
father stopped him and said, "What are you talking
about? Don't you know you're my son, and you'll
always be my son?" There's nothing you can do to
change the fact that you're a son. When you gave
your life to Christ, you were born into the family of God. You can't get unborn. You can't make
a mistake that's too big. You can't get too far off
course. You may disqualify yourself, but God never
disqualifies you.

Are you living like a slave when in fact you're
a son? Are you trying to convince God to hire you
back as a servant when God is saying, "Kill the fatted
calf. My son is home"? God has already received you
back into His family. But what if the son had turned
and said, "Dad, no. I can't accept your goodness. I
don't deserve it. Let me just work with the servants

to try to pay you back the inheritance I wasted"? That would have ruined the story. Yet how many of us are doing the same thing? We're not receiving God's goodness. We're beating ourselves up for our failures. We're letting the accuser convince us that we've somehow gone from a son to a slave.

I love the fact that when this son returned home, the father never brought up his past failures. He didn't say, "Okay, I'll let you come back, but you shouldn't have done that." God is not interested in your past. The enemy will work overtime trying to remind you of all your mistakes, making you feel guilty and unworthy. Don't believe those lies. You're not going to qualify as a son when you perform well enough. You're a son right now. You're a daughter right now. Why don't you come back into the family, start believing again, start dreaming again? You can start a party up in heaven. You can cause God to turn on the music and begin a celebration. When He sees you shake off a slave mentality and start having a son mentality, He says about you, "Go kill the fatted calf. We're going to have a party. My son, my daughter, has come back home."

> *You're not going to qualify as a son when you perform well enough.*

You Are Royalty

Many years ago, there was a man in Europe who saved up all his money to come to America. After months and months, he finally had just enough to purchase the ticket on a passenger ship. It was going to take two months to cross the ocean, so he brought a suitcase filled with the only food that he could afford—cheese and crackers. When the other passengers on the ship went to the beautiful dining room to have their fancy meals, he would go over into the corner and eat his cheese and crackers. This went on day after day, week after week. He could smell the delicious foods and wanted to join the other passengers so badly, but he just didn't have the resources. The last day of the trip, another passenger came over and said, "I can't help but notice that you're always over here eating cheese and crackers. Why don't you come in and have dinner with us?" The man was embarrassed and replied, "I saved up all my money, but I only had enough to buy the ticket. I didn't have enough to purchase the meals." The other passenger shook his head and said, "Didn't you realize the meals were included in the price of the ticket? You had the right to be in here with us the whole time."

I wonder how many of us are missing out on God's best because we don't realize the meals have been paid for. We're over in the corner, so to speak, like a servant eating cheese and crackers, when God is saying, "You're a son. You're a daughter. Step up to the table. I've paid the price. There's a place with your name on it." You may have made mistakes—forgiveness has been paid for, mercy has been paid for. You had bad breaks and people did you wrong—new beginnings have been paid for. Beauty for ashes belongs to you. Why don't you come on up to the table? You're struggling with your finances, and nobody in your family has gotten ahead. Don't be satisfied with cheese and crackers. Abundance has been paid for. New levels are in your future.

Sometimes what's holding us back is that we don't really know who we are. We think we're average, just ordinary, when in fact we are royalty. We are sons and daughters of the Most High God. When God breathed His

> *Sometimes what's holding us back is that we don't really know who we are.*

life into you, He crowned you with His favor. He put a robe of righteousness on you. He says, "You have been fearfully and wonderfully made." Don't go through life with a cheese-and-crackers mentality. Have a son mentality, an abundant mentality.

Step Up to Who You Were Created to Be

In Judges 6, an angel told Gideon that he was to go out and save the Israelites from the enemy army that was approaching. Gideon responded, "I can't do that. I come from the poorest family, and I am the least one in my father's house." He was saying, "You have the wrong person. I'm not at the dinner table. I'm eating cheese and crackers." He had a slave mentality: "I'm at a disadvantage." He didn't realize he was royalty. A few chapters later, when Gideon was talking with his defeated enemies about some fellow soldiers whom he was trying to find, he asked them what the men looked like. They said, "They looked like you, Gideon, like a king's son." Gideon had felt inadequate, as though he didn't measure up, but even his enemies could see he was a king's son.

You may feel as though you're at a disadvantage.

It's causing you to shrink back, to not pursue your dreams. Like Gideon, you may not be able to see it, but even the enemy knows you're royalty. Even

> *Why don't you put down the cheese and crackers and step up to who you were created to be?*

the enemy knows you are destined to do great things. Why don't you put down the cheese and crackers and step up to who you were created to be? You're no longer a slave, you're a son. You used to be a slave to fear, to addictions, to poverty, to depression, but you've been born into a new family and a new life.

When I think of you, through my eyes of faith I see a masterpiece, I see royalty. I don't see an average person. I don't see someone who is addicted. I don't see someone who is sick and weak. I don't see someone who is in poverty and lack. I see a blessed person, a victorious person, a favored person. I see a King's son, a King's daughter. Now, do your part, shake off the slave mentality, and start having a son mentality. If you'll do this, I believe and declare every chain that's holding you back is being broken. God is going to release healing, favor, breakthroughs, and abundance. You're going to rise higher and become everything He's created you to be.

CHAPTER SEVEN

Know You Are Loved

After Victoria and I had been dating for about nine months, a friend of mine called me secretly. She said, "Joel, I just talked to Victoria. Don't tell her that I called, but she told me she thinks she loves you!" My friend was so excited, and she was waiting for me to join in the excitement, but I had a problem with two words—*she thinks*. If *she thinks* she loves me, that could mean she does, or it could mean she doesn't. She's still trying to figure it out. It could go either way. *She thinks* didn't give me any confidence at all. In fact, it made me think, *I need to perform better. I need to do more and try to really impress her, or I might not be good enough. She thinks* put me under more pressure. Eventually, I'm happy to say that Victoria came to her senses, and she went from "I think" to "I know," and that was over thirty-one years ago.

When you *know* that somebody loves you, it puts you at ease. You don't have to try to perform, to impress, to be good enough. You can relax and be yourself. You're comfortable, you're secure. But a lot of people live with an "I *think* He loves me" mentality when it comes to God, because they base it on their performance. "I went to church last weekend. I did good. I think He loves me. I volunteered at the hospital. I was kind to my neighbor. I resisted temptation. I earned His love." The problem with this approach is that when we make mistakes, when we get off course, when we don't perform perfectly, we think God goes and finds somebody else to love. After all, human nature says, "If you don't love me, I'm not going to love you back." People often love you conditionally. If you do right, perform right, and treat them right, they will love you. If you let them down, they'll go find somebody else. But God is not like that. When we make mistakes, God doesn't change His mind about us. If you run away from God, instead of turning the other way, God will come running

> *Human nature says, "If you don't love me, I'm not going to love you back."*

toward you. Quit trying to earn His love. There's nothing you can do to make God love you any more or any less. It's a gift. Just receive it by faith.

Sometimes we're trying to clean ourselves up, trying hard to be good enough, and then we'll believe that God really loves us. But take the pressure off. God loves you right now. He loved you when you were doing wrong. He loved you when you were off course. The apostle Paul says that *nothing* can separate us from the love of God. You are a marked man, a marked woman. God put His love on you. Now you are permanently loved. The psalmist says, "If I go down to the depths of the ocean, God, You are there. If I go up to the heavens, God, You are still there." You can't get away from His love. "Well, Joel, I'm an atheist. I don't believe in God." He still loves you. "I've made mistakes. I've had a rough past." *Nothing* you've done has changed God's love. "I have an addiction. I still struggle with my temper." That doesn't cancel His love for you.

Get Rid of the "I Think" Mentality

The Scripture speaks of "the great love with which God loved us." It wasn't a little love, an "I think" love, or a conditional love. It was and is a great love. We think about how much we love God, but what's far more profound is how much God loves us. Before you were formed in your mother's womb, God knew you. He took time to plan out all your days. He knows your thoughts before you think them. He knows your words before you speak them. Jesus says "the very hairs of your head are all numbered." Now, I love Victoria, but I have never taken the time to number her hairs. To number doesn't mean there are 54,623 hairs—that's counting. To number means that each hair has its own number, such as "this is hair number 21,238." Every time you lose a single hair, God has to renumber.

There was a popular self-improvement book published some years ago that was adapted into a movie called *He's Just Not That Into You.* It was about guys not really liking a girl and how the girl shouldn't waste her time. Can I tell you that God is just the opposite? He's way into you. If He's taking the time to number your hairs, to know your thoughts, to plan out all your days, do you really think there's anything you can do to cause Him to stop loving you? So how must God feel when we go around thinking, *I think He loves me. I think I'm good enough. I think I haven't done too much wrong*? Get rid of the "I think" mentality and start having an "I know" mentality. It's very freeing when you can say, "I know that God loves me. I know that I'm the apple of His eye. I know that He's smiling down on me." Voices will whisper, "No, not you, not ever. You've made mistakes. You lose your temper. You're not religious enough." God doesn't love you because you're religious, or you're good enough, or you come from a certain family. He loves you because you are His child. He breathed His life into you. When you receive His love, you'll

> *When you go from "I think" to "I know," you'll quit trying to earn His love.*

live with a confidence. When you go from "I think" to "I know," you'll quit trying to earn His love. You'll quit trying to be good enough. You'll live securely, knowing that your heavenly Father loves you.

In the Bible, the book of John was written by the disciple John. What's interesting is that within this book he never refers to himself as John. When he talks about himself, instead of using his name, he says, "The disciple whom Jesus loved." In John 13, he wrote, "The disciple whom Jesus loved was sitting next to Jesus." He could have simply written, "John was sitting next to Jesus." When Matthew, Mark, and Luke wrote their books, their accounts of the gospel, they referred to themselves by using their own names. Can you imagine if they had read John's account? They would've thought, *Who does John think he is, describing himself as the one whom Jesus loved? Jesus loved us all. The nerve of that guy.*

But John had an incredible confidence not just in how much he loved God, but in how much God loved him. Five times he referred to himself as the disciple whom Jesus loved. You would think, *All right, John, we got it the first time. We heard you loud and clear. You think you're the one whom He loves, and you don't have to keep telling us.* But in chapter 19, John wrote again, "When Jesus saw His mother, and the disciple whom Jesus loved standing by." Now, you know that Jesus loved His mother. In fact, He probably loved His mother more than He loved John. But John didn't take the time to tell us how much Jesus loved His mother, he just reiterated the fact that he was the one whom Jesus loved. Some may fault John for it, but I have to give him credit. John knew how much he was loved. Two chapters later, John wrote, "The disciple whom Jesus loved said to Peter." John didn't say, "The disciple whom Jesus loved said to the other disciple whom Jesus loved." You could take this as being arrogant and self-centered, but John was showing us the confidence he had in how much he knew God loved him. When you can do as John did—maybe not announce it to everybody, and don't put it on your business card—you can say in your heart, "I'm the one whom He loves." You can wake up in the morning and say, "Good morning, Lord. It's me, the one whom You love." All through the day you can say, "Lord, I love You, and I know I'm the one whom You love."

You Are the One Whom He Loves

In Chapter Three I mentioned that when Lazarus was very sick and close to death, his two sisters, Mary and Martha, sent a message to their good friend Jesus, asking Him to come and pray for Lazarus. Jesus was in another city at the time. The message didn't say, "Jesus, we're begging You to please come and pray for Lazarus. You know that Lazarus is a good man. You know how much he loves You." Instead, the message was, "Jesus, the one whom You love is sick." They didn't tell Jesus how much Lazarus loved Him. They thought it would be more persuasive, more effective, to remind Jesus about how much He loved Lazarus.

Sometimes we're trying to convince God that we love Him. "God, I went to church last week. God, I bit my tongue at the office when I felt like telling them off. God, I've been performing so well. Would You please help me now?" Why don't you do as Mary and Martha did and say, "Lord, the one whom You love needs healing. The one whom You love is lonely. The one whom You love has a child who's off course." What moves God is not just your love for Him, but recognizing His love for you. It pleases God when you know you are dearly loved. That's why the Scripture says, "Come boldly to the throne." Don't go to Him feeling unworthy.

> *What moves God is not just your love for Him, but recognizing His love for you.*

If my son came to me embarrassed and ashamed, with his head down, and he said, "Dad, I hate to bother you. I know you're busy. I don't deserve it. It's just little old me, but Dad, I'm begging you, would you help me in this area?" I wouldn't feel sorry for him; I would feel badly about myself. As a father, I would think, *What have I done wrong? How can my own son come to me feeling so inferior and unworthy, begging me for a little help?* It's not my lack of love for my son, because I'd give him the world. It's his lack of knowing how much he is loved. Now, I'm happy to say that my children don't feel that way. They know how much they're loved, and they're not afraid to ask.

When our daughter, Alexandra, was ten years old, she was about to go out to eat and then go ice skating with her cousins. She came to me in the den and said, "Dad, can I have twenty dollars to go out?" I said, "Sure, go back and get it off my bathroom counter where I keep my keys." She gave me a kiss and said, "Thank you." Then she turned and started walking toward the garage, which was the wrong way. I said, "Wait a minute! Aren't you going to get the money?" She smiled and said, "I already did. I knew you would say yes." That made me feel good as a father. She knows how much I love her. She's not living with an "I think" mentality. She's not saying, "I hope Dad loves me. If I perform well enough, he'll love me." She has no doubt: "My father loves me."

What if we felt the same way about our heavenly Father? If you want to make God's day, start approaching Him like you know He loves you, like you know He's for you, like you know He's longing to be good to you. It doesn't bring God any pleasure when we go around feeling insecure and unworthy and beating ourselves up for past mistakes. Shake that off and start going boldly to the throne.

You Are His Favorite

Alexandra is in college now. She called Victoria one day and explained that their sorority was having their big mother-daughter weekend, and she wanted to make sure that Victoria could come. When she gave Victoria the dates, Victoria said, "Oh, Alexandra, we have a Night of Hope on that Friday night, plus your dad and I are supposed to speak at Lakewood that weekend, and he really doesn't like me to miss." Alexandra said, "Oh, Mom, don't worry. I'll call Dad. He'll do anything I ask." Needless to say, Victoria attended Alexandra's event. Do you know why Alexandra could have that boldness? It's because she knows she's the one whom I love. She knows she's my prized possession. She knows I'll go out of my way to be good to her. She's my child. Now, I'll be good, kind, loving, and generous to other people's children. But I have to be honest: if it's between *another* child and *my* child, I'm going to choose my child. She's my daughter. She's my favorite.

That's the way God feels about you. You're His child. Can I tell you a secret? You are His favorite. You're the one whom He loves. I've heard it said that God has no favorites. I think that's wrong. God has all favorites. He's not like us in that way. He doesn't have to pick and choose, because He has unlimited love. He doesn't just show love, He doesn't just express love—He is love. Love is not just what He does; it is Who He is.

> I've heard it said that God has no favorites. I think that's wrong. God has all favorites.

When you start seeing yourself as His favorite, you'll go to Him with confidence, you'll pray bold prayers, you'll ask Him for your dreams, you'll believe for your health to turn around, you'll expect new doors to open, you'll move up to the next level—not because of who you are, but because of Who your Father is. You know He'll go out of His way to be good to you.

I grew up with five siblings. My sister April is

the youngest. She always felt as though she was the favorite of the family. The truth is, my parents had more resources when she came along. From a young age, April started telling us that she was our parents' favorite. Now, that never bothered me because I knew she wasn't the favorite—I was. But she's been doing this for so long that now when my mother sends us kids a group text, it lists our names at the top: "Paul, Lisa, Tamara, Joel." But instead of "April," it says "Favorite." I had to use my mother's cell phone one time, and under the contacts I noticed that she has April stored as "Favorite." Now, that's not right!

I can imagine that if God had a cell phone, you would be stored under "Favorite." It wouldn't be "Joseph Rodriguez," but rather "Favorite Rodriguez." It would be "Favorite Smith," "Favorite Edward," and "Favorite Rebecca." We're all His favorite. You're the one whom He loves. "Well, not me, Joel. You don't know the mistakes I've made. You don't know the past I've lived. When I clean myself up, I know God will love me a lot more." Nothing you can do will make God love you more. You might as well believe that you are His favorite right now. He may not be pleased with all your behavior, but that doesn't change His love for you. You may have made mistakes,

you may have shortcom-
ings, but He's still proud
of you. He still says you're
amazing. He still calls you
a masterpiece. Knowing
that you're loved is what
will give you the strength
to do better and to break
any chains that are holding you back.

> *Knowing that you're loved is what will give you the strength to do better and to break any chains that are holding you back.*

You Are Invited to Come

In Luke 19 is the story of a tax collector named
Zacchaeus who lived in Jericho. Back in those days,
tax collectors were known for being dishonest, for
cheating people. They were not just disliked, they
were hated. Zacchaeus was the chief tax collector,
which meant he was especially despised and looked
down upon by everyone—not just figuratively, but
even physically, for he was very short. One day Jesus
was passing through Jericho and word spread quickly.
People, including Zacchaeus, went out to try to get a
glimpse of Jesus. But it was so crowded, there were
so many throngs of people, that Zacchaeus couldn't

see Jesus because he was too short. Rather than give up, he ran ahead and climbed up in a tree. He was in perfect position, had a great viewpoint. After a few minutes, Jesus came walking down the street. I can imagine that Zacchaeus was in awe. He had heard how Jesus had healed the sick, opened blind eyes, and cured the lepers. Now Jesus was passing right in front of him. It was an amazing moment, with hundreds of people trying to touch Jesus and get His attention.

All of a sudden, in the midst of the commotion, Jesus stopped. Everyone froze, thinking, *Why is He stopping?* They got quiet, and someone whispered, "He's going to say something." Jesus turned and looked up in the tree, and in that moment time stopped for Zacchaeus. Every eye was focused on him. Zacchaeus knew he was hated and despised by all these people whom he had cheated. He was waiting for Jesus to condemn him, but Jesus said, "Zacchaeus, come down from the tree. I want to go to your house and have dinner." When he heard those words, I believe Zacchaeus felt something he had never felt. Something on the inside said, "Zacchaeus, you're the one whom He loves." Among the crowd of people gathered that day, there were no doubt rabbis, elders from the synagogue, and other highly respected leaders. Jesus could have gone to dinner with any of them, but He was making this point: You don't have to

> *When he heard those words, I believe Zacchaeus felt something he had never felt.*

have it all together for God to love you. You don't have to first clean yourself up, and then you can come down out of the tree and go to dinner. If that was the case, none of us have a chance.

What's interesting is that the name Zacchaeus means "pure one." I doubt if anyone in that crowd ever called him Zacchaeus. They probably called him "fraud," "crook," or "cheater." One version says they called him "scum." Jesus could have looked up in the tree and said, "Hey, you! Come down. Hey, mister. Hey, sir." But Jesus purposefully said, "Zacchaeus, pure one, come down. I want to go to your house for dinner." The religious leaders nearly passed out. They said, "Why would He go to dinner with such a notorious sinner?" We don't see people the way God sees them. We look at their behavior, how perfectly they perform. God looks beyond all that. They saw a notorious sinner; God saw the one whom He loved.

You may have made mistakes, you may have gotten

off course as Zacchaeus had, you know that you're not where you should be. But if Jesus was passing by today, He wouldn't say, "Hey, Joel, come on, let's go to lunch. You pastor that big church. Hey, Sister Do Right, you haven't made a mistake in thirty years. I'm proud of you. You're so good. Let's go get something to eat." He would pass by all the people who look as though they have it together, and He would come to you. You're the one whom He loves. You may be up in the tree trying to hide, while you're dealing with issues. Can I tell you we all have issues? God is saying, "Come down, pure one. Come down, forgiven child. Come down, redeemed daughter. Come down, favorite one."

Jesus' point in choosing Zacchaeus over all the other "good" people that day was to let you know that your performance doesn't determine God's love for you. "Well, Joel, if I can break this bad habit, if I can stop this addiction, I know He'll love me a lot more." He will be more pleased with your behavior, and your life will go better, but that doesn't affect God's love for you. He's calling you "pure one" right now. Will you receive His love? Will you come down and go to dinner, so to speak? Or are you going to stay up in the tree and let condemning voices con-

vince that you're all
washed up? You have to
shake that off and say it
by faith: "Lord, I believe
I'm the one whom You

> *He's calling you "pure one" right now. Will you receive His love?*

love. Despite my failures, despite my mistakes, I believe You still have a great plan for my life."

This Is Real Love

First John 4:10 says, "This is real love—not that we loved God, but that He loved us and sent His Son as a sacrifice to take away our sins." Real love is not our love for God, it's God's love for us. When we try to perform to gain His love, the problem is that we can never measure up. There will always be something we can't do right, some reason we can't feel good about ourselves. Why don't you take the pressure off and receive real love, God's love for you?

That's what the lady who was caught in the act of adultery had to do in John 8. The religious leaders brought her to Jesus, threw her at His feet, and said, "Teacher, in the law Moses commanded us to stone such women. What do You say we should do?" Jesus answered, "You who are without sin throw the first stone." Starting with the oldest ones first, they all left. Jesus asked the woman, "Where are your accusers? Hasn't anyone condemned you?" She said, "No one, Lord." He said, "Neither do I condemn you; go and sin no more." He didn't say, "Go and sin no more, and then I won't condemn you. Change your ways, get your act together, quit giving in to the temptation, and then I'll love you, then I'll be for you." Just the opposite. He first said, "I don't condemn you." Before He talked about her behavior, before he addressed the issues, Jesus wanted to make sure she knew she was the one whom He loved.

When she felt this real love, when she realized the one person who could have condemned her wouldn't do it, I believe something happened on the inside. She walked out of the temple a changed woman. Sometimes religion tells us, "Clean yourself up, then God will love you. If you fail to do what's right, if you don't perform correctly, God won't have anything to do with you. If you're good enough, if you measure up, then God will help you." That's not real love; that's conditional love. Real love is not about your performance, what you do or don't do. It's about what God has already done. It's not based on how much you love God; it's based on how much God loves you.

Real love is not about your performance, what you do or don't do.

His Face Is toward You

When my brother, Paul, was a little boy, before any of us siblings were born, my parents would put him in his bed at night, and then they would go and get in their own bed. Their rooms were just a few feet apart, down a short hallway. My father would always say, "Good night, Paul," and Paul would answer back, "Good night, Daddy. Good night, Mother." One night, for some reason, Paul was a little afraid. A couple minutes after they had said their good-nights, Paul said, "Daddy, are you still in there?" My father said, "Yes, Paul, I'm still here." It was quiet for a few seconds, then Paul asked, "Daddy, is your face turned toward me?" My father said, "Yes, Paul, my face is turned toward you." Somehow, it made Paul feel better just knowing that our father's face was turned toward him.

Can I tell you that your heavenly Father's face is always turned toward you? You're the one whom He loves. You're His favorite child. He's not counting your mistakes against you; He's calling you "pure one." Receive His love. All through the day, say, "Lord, thank You that I'm the one whom You love. Thank You that Your face is turned toward me." Remember, real love is not about your love for God; it's recognizing the great love God has for you.

CHAPTER EIGHT

Approve Yourself

Too many people go around feeling as though something is wrong on the inside. They don't really like who they are. They focus on their faults and weaknesses. They're constantly critical toward themselves. There's a recording of everything they've done wrong that is always playing in their mind: "You're impatient. You blew your diet yesterday. You lost your temper. You're still struggling with that addiction. You should be ashamed of yourself." They wonder why they're unhappy and don't realize it's because they have a war going on inside. But you're not supposed to go through life feeling wrong about yourself. Quit focusing on your faults. Quit overanalyzing your weaknesses. Quit beating yourself up because you're not where you thought you would be.

Next level thinking says you're not a finished product. God is still working on you. The Scripture speaks of how God changes us from glory to glory. You have to learn to enjoy the glory you're in right now. You may have some weaknesses—we all do. There may be some areas where you know you need to improve, but being down on yourself is not going to help you do better. Having that nagging feeling that tells you, "You don't measure up. God's not pleased with you. You'll never get it right," is not going to help you move forward. You have to accept yourself right where you are, faults and all. God is the Potter, we are the clay. He's the one Who is making and molding you. It may not be happening as fast as you would like, but you don't control the timetable. Will you trust Him in the process? Will you accept yourself in the glory you're in right now?

The problem with not liking yourself is that you're the only person whom you can never get away from. You can get away from your boss, you can get away from your neighbor, you can get away from that crazy uncle, but you can never get away from you. You wake up with you, you take a shower with you, you go to work with you, and you even go on vacations with you. If you don't like you, your life is going to

be very miserable. Don't
go around being against
yourself. You may have
some things wrong with
you, but you have a lot
more things right with
you. You may have a long

> *The problem with not liking yourself is that you're the only person whom you can never get away from.*

way to go, but if you look back, you'll see how far
you've already come.

You're on the Potter's Wheel

Keep your flaws in perspective. Every person has
something they're dealing with. You may see someone who looks further along than you. They look
as though they have it all together. They're happy,
enjoying their life, but you need to realize they're
on the Potter's wheel. The reason they're not upset
and not down on themselves is they've learned this
principle—to enjoy where they are while God is in
the process of changing them. We think, *I'm going
to feel good about myself as soon as I lose these ten
pounds, as soon as I break this addiction, as soon as I
can control my mouth. Then I'll get rid of the guilt,*

the heaviness and condemnation. I'm asking you to feel good about yourself right where you are. If you don't understand this, you will go through life not liking yourself, because as soon as you overcome one weakness and cross it off your list, God will show you something else that you need to improve. It will be a never-ending cycle.

I talked to a man recently who said, "Joel, you're so calm and good-natured. Do you ever get upset? Do you ever lose your temper?" This is an area that I've never struggled in. I've always been easygoing. My mother tells people that she's never seen me angry a day in my life. God gives us grace in different areas. When I told him that, he shook his head and said, "I don't know what's wrong with me. I get upset so easily. I've been this way for my whole life." I told him what I'm telling you. As long as you're down on yourself, feeling as though you don't measure up and can't get it right, that's not only going to keep you from enjoying your life, it's

> *As long as you're down on yourself, feeling as though you don't measure up and can't get it right, that's not only going to keep you from enjoying your life, it's going to keep you from improving.*

going to keep you from improving. You have to give yourself a break. You're on the Potter's wheel. You can't change yourself. God has to give you the grace to change. It takes a mature person to accept who you are, to be at peace on the inside even though you have some areas where you need to improve.

It's easy to stay negative toward yourself, to be down when you can't get it right. But when you make the decision to accept yourself, faults and all, instead of beating yourself up, you have the attitude, *I'm not perfect. I have some areas in which I need to improve. But God, I want to thank You for the glory I'm in right now. I know You're the Potter. I'm going to stay on this wheel and keep being my best, knowing on Your timetable that You will change me.* This is the attitude that allows God to work.

The Scripture says in Hebrews 12:2, "Looking away from all that will distract and focusing our eyes on Jesus, the author and finisher of our faith." You have to look away from your faults, look away from your shortcomings. Focusing on your weaknesses will distract you from your purpose. Always thinking about how you don't measure up will distract you from the good things God has in store. This doesn't mean we don't try to improve. It means you don't let

> *It's okay to feel good about who you are while you're in the process of changing.*

that heaviness weigh you down to where you think there's something wrong with you. One of the worst mistakes you can make is to go through life being against yourself. Some people live with that nagging feeling that's always telling them, "You're not attractive enough. You're not disciplined enough. You still have that addiction. You'll never get it right." They've heard that playing in their minds for so long that it's become normal. Why don't you turn off that negative recording? Why don't you quit thinking about everything that's wrong with you and start thinking about what's right with you? You may have some areas in which you still struggle—join the crowd, we all do. No one is perfect. It's okay to feel good about who you are while you're in the process of changing.

Be Happy with Who You Are

The other day somebody asked me to name the one thing I would change about myself if I could. I don't mean to sound arrogant, but I couldn't think of anything. Now, there are plenty of areas in which I need and want to improve, but here's my point: I don't sit around thinking about everything that's wrong with me. I don't have all my flaws, weaknesses, and shortcomings at the forefront of my mind. I don't go through the day reliving my failures, beating myself up for past mistakes, or letting a negative recording condemn me for everything that I'm not. I say this with humility: "I like myself. I'm happy with who I am. I'm proud of who God made me to be." Again, I'm not bragging on me, I'm bragging on the goodness of God. I know that I'm the apple of His eye. I know that I'm a masterpiece. I know that I'm His prized possession, fearfully and wonderfully made.

And, yes, I have shortcomings, but I'm on the Potter's wheel. I'm a work in progress. God has His own timetable. While He's changing me, I'm going to feel good about who I am. I'm going to keep my head held high and enjoy my life, knowing that God will get me to where I'm supposed to be. It's very powerful when you can say, "I like who I am. I feel good about myself. I'm proud of who God made me to be." Most people can't do this. They say, "I would feel good about myself if I didn't have these weaknesses. I would be happy with who I am if I were a better parent, if I were more patient, if I weren't so jealous. I would hold my head high if I hadn't made these mistakes, if I hadn't blown that relationship." There will always be some reason why you won't feel good about who you are. The accuser will make sure to remind you of something you're not doing right, some area in which you're not up to par, some way that you failed. If you're going to live in victory, you have to put your foot down and say, "That's it. I'm done being against myself. I'm done feeling wrong on the inside. I'm done focusing on my weaknesses. I know I'm a child of the Most High God. I am redeemed, restored, and forgiven. God is taking me from glory to glory, so I'm going to look away from all that distracts. And I'm going to enjoy the glory I'm in right now."

Now, when you do this, don't be surprised if every voice tells you, "You're a hypocrite. You can't feel good about yourself. You still struggle, you still have that weakness." This is when you must have the boldness to say, "Yes, that's true, but I'm on the Potter's wheel. I'm growing and I'm changing. In the meantime, I feel good about me." Your destiny is too important to let that heaviness weigh you down. Your time is too valuable to be sitting around thinking about every-thing that's wrong with you. That's taking away your joy, your energy, your creativity, and your anointing. Start looking away from all of that. You're on the Potter's wheel. You're not going to change overnight. It's going to happen little by little.

But if you're always down on yourself because you think you're not far enough along and you're not growing as fast as you would like, you'll live frustrated. It's very freeing when you can be happy with who you are even though you have some areas in which you still need to improve. Think about the apostle Paul. He said, "The things I want to do, I don't do. The things I don't want to do, I end up doing." Even he wasn't perfect. He still struggled in some areas.

> *It's very freeing when you can be happy with who you are even though you have some areas in which you still need to improve.*

If the apostle Paul had lived down on himself, thinking, *Why can't I get it right?* he wouldn't have written almost half of the books of the New Testament. He wouldn't have become one of the heroes of faith. He didn't have it all together, and you don't have to have it all together in order to do something great. If you're waiting till you overcome all your weaknesses, till you perform perfectly, and then you're going to feel good about yourself, you'll be waiting your whole life. There are some weaknesses that God leaves on purpose so we have to depend on Him. Otherwise, we would think we could do it all in our own strength. Why don't you start feeling good about yourself right where you are? If Paul could accomplish all that he did with his flaws and weaknesses, you can accomplish your dreams with what you're dealing with.

You Are Already Approved

When you're on the Potter's wheel, you have to be pliable. When you're at peace with yourself, you are the easiest to work with. You are not upset, angry on the inside, or disappointed because you're not where you think you should be. All that does is slow down the process. The right attitude is, *I may have some things wrong with me, but I'm at peace. I know I'm on the way. I'm in the process. And what God started in my life, He's going to finish.*

Jeremiah 1 says, "Before you were formed in your mother's womb, God knew you and approved you." It doesn't say, "He approves you as long as you don't make any mistakes. He approves you as long as you perform perfectly, as

> *The right attitude is,* I may have some things wrong with me, but I'm at peace. I know I'm on the way. I'm in the process.

long as you don't have any weaknesses." He approved you before you were formed in your mother's womb. This means He approves you with those weaknesses. He approves you despite those shortcomings. You're not a surprise to God. He knows the end from the beginning. He knew every area in which you would ever struggle. That's why He has you on the Potter's wheel. That's why He's changing you from glory to glory. You're not defective, you're not a mistake. When God created you, He called you a masterpiece. He stepped back and said, "That was very good."

You may have flaws and weaknesses. Those voices will try to convince you to live feeling down on yourself, thinking, *God's not going to bless me. You don't know what I struggle with. I'll never get it right.*

Don't believe those lies. Before you showed up on planet earth, God already approved you. Since God approves you, why don't you start approving yourself? Why don't you start feeling good about who you are? A lot of times we think we can't feel good about ourselves until we do everything right. If we resist the temptation, if we bite our tongue, if we're more patient, then we believe God will approve us and be pleased. But the truth is, there's nothing you can do to make God love you more. His approval is not based on your performance, it's based on your relationship. He handpicked you. He chose you before you could choose Him.

When you understand that the Creator of the universe approves you, you won't go around being down on yourself because you're not where you thought you should be, trying to gain God's approval by performing perfectly, never making a mistake. You know you already have His approval. This takes the pressure off. You can relax knowing you're on the Potter's wheel, that He's making and molding you. When those condemning thoughts come and try to push you down, saying, "You're not far enough along. You should feel bad about yourself," you can say, "No, thanks. I know that God approves me, so I'm going to approve myself. I'm going to feel good about who I am."

Put On Your Breastplate

The apostle Paul says in the book of Ephesians to put on the breastplate of God's approval. Every morning when you get up, you should say, "Father, thank You that You approve me. Thank You that You are pleased with me." You have to put it on. It's not going to happen automatically. Thoughts will try to convince you that you don't deserve God's blessing: *You made that mistake last week. You still struggle with your temper. You failed yesterday.* If you're not putting His approval on, you'll start living with guilt, feeling unworthy, as though you don't deserve God's blessing.

This is the reason many people live with the heaviness, that feeling that there's something wrong with them—they're not putting on the breastplate of God's approval. It's a breastplate, meaning that it covers the most important area of your life, which is your heart. You may have many areas in which you still struggle, but being against yourself is not going to help you do better. Living condemned, feeling as though you're unworthy and don't deserve God's blessing, is going to cause you to get stuck. You have to put on His approval. All through the day in your thoughts be saying, "God is pleased with me. He's at work in my life. I'm not perfect, but I'm forgiven. I have these weaknesses, but I'm on the Potter's wheel. He's making me, He's molding me. I'm coming up to a higher level." Thoughts will say, "You can't feel good about yourself. You still struggle in that area." Just answer back, "Yes, that's true, but God's approval is not based on how good I am. It's based on how good He is. He approved me before I showed up. He accepted me despite my shortcomings, so I'm going to start putting on His approval."

> *You may have many areas in which you still struggle, but being against yourself is not going to help you do better.*

After Jesus was baptized in the Jordan River by John the Baptist, a voice boomed out of the heavens, saying, "This is My beloved Son, in whom I am well pleased." What's interesting is that up to this point in Jesus' life, He hadn't performed one miracle. He hadn't opened any blind eyes, hadn't turned water into wine, hadn't raised Lazarus from the dead. Yet His

Father said, "I am well pleased with Him." It's the same principle: God was pleased with Jesus because of Who He was and not because of anything He had done.

We think, *If I can get rid of this bad habit, if I can bite my tongue and not argue so much, if I can be more disciplined in what I watch, then God will be pleased with me.* The fact is that God is well pleased with you right now. He may not be pleased with all your behavior, but He is pleased with you. He's already approved you. He's already called you a masterpiece. But if you listen to the condemning voices that tell you that you don't measure up and you'll never get it right, you'll start living condemned, feeling guilty and wrong on the inside. Why don't you start putting on His approval, knowing that God is well pleased with you? A lot of people think just the opposite—that God is out to get them, that He's waiting for them to make the next mistake so He can push them down even further. That's not how our God is. You need to go through the day saying, "Father, thank You that You are pleased with me. Thank You that You have approved me. Thank You that You've already accepted me." When thoughts tell you, "Who do you think you are?" just answer back, "I'm a child of the

Most High God. I am redeemed, restored, accepted, and approved."

Are you putting on your breastplate of approval, or are you wearing rags of condemnation, unworthiness, and guilt? Do you believe that God is well pleased with you, or are you trying to gain His approval by performing perfectly? As parents, we know that our children make mistakes and have weaknesses. But we also know they're growing, they're learning, they're making progress. If you were to ask me if I were pleased with my children, the first thing I would not do is make a list of all their mistakes. I wouldn't tell you what they've done wrong over the past three months. I wouldn't have to think twice about my answer. I would say, "Yes, I am very pleased. They're great children." I would make a list of everything I like about them. They're loving, kind, talented, and fun. That's the way God thinks of you. He's not focusing on your faults, looking at everything you've done wrong, making a list of your shortcomings. He's focusing on what you're doing right. He's looking at how you're growing, how

> *Are you putting on your breastplate of approval, or are you wearing rags of condemnation, unworthiness, and guilt?*

you're making progress, how you're not where you used to be. Don't go through life feeling wrong on the inside. Take off the rags of unworthiness and start putting on your breastplate of God's approval.

"As You Love Yourself"

The most important relationship you have is your relationship with yourself. If you don't get along with yourself, you won't be able to get along with anybody else. It will affect every relationship, including your relationship with God. If you're living under guilt, feeling condemned and unworthy, you won't go to God with boldness. You won't ask Him for your dreams. The reason that many people can't get along with others is because they don't like themselves. They're insecure, they're bitter, they're defensive, and it spills over into their relationships. Jesus says, "Love your neighbor as you love yourself." You can't love your neighbor if you don't first love yourself. You can't give away something you don't have. If you don't have a healthy respect for yourself, if you're not putting on His approval each day, knowing that you're a masterpiece, knowing that you're made in

> *You can't love your neighbor if you don't first love yourself. You can't give away something you don't have.*

the image of God, then you'll start focusing on your faults and shortcomings. You'll end up feeling insecure and inferior. That will cause you to struggle in relationships.

The Scripture says our faith is made effective when we acknowledge everything good. If you're acknowledging everything you don't like about yourself—your flaws, your shortcomings, your failures—your faith is not going to be effective. That's going to cause you to get stuck. You have enough to overcome in life as it is. Don't be against yourself. Quit taking inventory of everything you don't like. Sometimes we spend more time looking at what's wrong with us than we do looking at what's right with us. It should be just the opposite. Start acknowledging the good. Let me help you start right now. You're reading this book—that's good. You were patient in traffic last week—that was good. You were kind to that stranger—that was good. You overlooked that insult—that was good. There's a lot right about you.

Even physically, we tend to focus on what we

don't like and say, "I'm so old and wrinkled. I wish I were taller. Where did my hair go?" Turn it around. Instead of being critical, say, "I am fearfully and wonderfully made. I am one of a kind. I am a masterpiece." Something powerful happens when you say, "I like who I am. I'm not perfect, and I have some shortcomings, but I'm growing, I'm changing. And since God approves me, I'm going to approve myself." When you do this, chains are broken in the unseen realm—chains of guilt, chains of low self-esteem, chains of inferiority. When you are for yourself, you are in agreement with God.

Some people have never once said, "I like myself. I like my gifts. I like my personality. I like my looks. I'm happy with who God made me to be." You may say, "Well, Joel, I'm not going to say I like myself. That's weird." But if you don't like yourself in a healthy way, other people are not going to like you. You project what you believe on the inside. If you feel wrong about yourself, you will project inferiority, unfriendliness, and discontentment to others. I'm asking you to feel good about who you are. You may not be where you want to be, but you're on the way. God is changing you from glory to glory. Start enjoying the glory that you're in right now. You may have some weaknesses—we all do. Don't you dare go through life being against yourself.

God is saying today, "You are My beloved son, My beloved daughter, in whom I am well pleased." Now do your part. Start putting on the breastplate of God's approval each morning. If you do this, I believe and declare every chain that's holding you back is being broken. God is going to keep making and molding you. You're going to come up higher, overcome obstacles, and reach the fullness of your destiny.

CHAPTER NINE

Get the Contaminants Out

I don't know about you, but I've found bitterness is always knocking at the door—people do you wrong, you didn't get the promotion, you came down with an illness. You can't stop difficult things from happening to you, but you can choose how you respond to them. If you hold on to the hurt and dwell on the offense, thinking, *Why did they say that about me? Why did I lose my loved one? Why did that friend walk away?*, then you open the door to bitterness. When you're bitter, it affects every area of your life. Bitterness poisons your attitude to the point where you see everything in a negative light. You can't enjoy life; there's always something wrong.

Bitter people don't have good relationships and are easily offended. They'll jump down your throat for the smallest thing. It's the bitterness coming out. You may have a good reason to be bitter, maybe something happened that was unfair and hurt you, but holding on to it is only going to make it worse. It's going to steal your dreams and rob you of your joy. Bitterness can keep you from your destiny.

I know people who are still bitter over something that happened thirty years ago. They're bitter because they were mistreated growing up or because a relationship didn't work out. You have to let it go. God sees what's happening to you. He knows what wasn't fair, He knows who walked away, and He knows how to make it up to you. He knows how to bring you out better. Let it go and trust Him to be your vindicator. The longer you hold on to it, the harder it is to get rid of it. The more you dwell on it, the more you relive it, the more you let it bother you, the deeper it gets rooted in you. The key is to forgive quickly. When something unfair happens that you don't understand and the question "Why did this happen?" comes up, let go of it quickly. When you feel the bitterness trying to take

> *The more you dwell on it, the more you relive it, the more you let it bother you, the deeper it gets rooted in you.*

root, right then say, "God, I'm turning this over to You. I know that You are my vindicator. I know that You'll make my wrongs right. You said You would give me beauty for these ashes."

Guard Your Heart

Here's how bitterness tries to get inside. When you don't get the contract you work so hard for, bitterness will come and say, "That's not fair. Go ahead and have a chip on your shoulder." When the medical report isn't what you want, bitterness will show up and say, "You prayed and you believed, so why didn't God answer your prayer?" At the office a coworker says something to try to make you look bad in front of your boss. It starts off as a small offense, not a big deal, just a little seed. If you choose to ignore it and let it go, nothing will come of it. But if you dwell on it, if you start thinking of how you can pay them back, the next time you see them you'll give them the cold shoulder. Now that little seed is taking root. Before long, it will grow and pollute other areas of your life.

That's why it says in Hebrews, "Make sure that

no root of bitterness springs forth and causes trouble and many become contaminated by it." Notice that bitterness is described as a root. You can't see a root; it's hidden, it's underground. But here's the problem: A bitter root produces bitter fruit. If you have a root of bitterness, it will contaminate your life.

I know a young man who felt as though he'd been treated unfairly by his employer and became disgruntled. He eventually moved to another state, but over the years he never let it go. He became more and more offended, kept talking about it, bringing up all the ways he wasn't treated right. His boss had actually been generous and kind to him in many ways. There were just little things that this young man kept dwelling on, blowing them out of proportion. Because he wouldn't let it go, those small offenses turned into a root of bitterness. Whereas he used to be happy and fun to be around, now he's sour and has a chip on his shoulder. It's affecting his relationships. It's affecting his career.

Proverbs says, "Guard your heart with all diligence, for out of it flow the issues of life." One of our most important responsibilities is to keep our heart pure. Life is too short for you to live offended, not forgiving, bitter over what didn't work out. You have to guard your heart. It's easy to let what's on the outside get on the inside. It takes discipline to say, "I'm not going to dwell on that offense. I'm not going to feel sorry for myself because something didn't work out." You only have so much emotional energy each day. It's not an unlimited supply. Do

> *It's easy to let what's on the outside get on the inside.*

you know how much energy it takes to hold a grudge, to go around offended? That's wasting valuable energy that you need for your dreams, for your children, and for your destiny. Quit letting what's on the outside get on the inside; start guarding your heart.

The apostle Paul had many opportunities to live offended. He said in his last letter to Timothy, "Alexander the coppersmith did me great wrongs, but that is no concern of mine. I know God will pay him back." That's a mature attitude. "Somebody did me great wrong, but I'm not upset, and I won't let bitterness in or carry a chip on my shoulder. I know God is fighting my battles. I know God will be my vindicator."

Examine Your Roots

It's interesting that while we can't see a tree's roots, the roots are where the tree gets its life. We see the outside—the leaves, the branches, and the trunk—but the roots are what feed the tree. When your roots are healthy, positive, and hopeful, that's feeding you with life, strength, encouragement, and hope. The problem is that if you have bitter roots, you're not being fed the right nutrients. You wonder why you don't have any energy, why you don't laugh anymore, why you don't dream like you used to—it's because those bitter roots are feeding you bitterness, self-pity, and anger. That's draining all the life, the strength, the passion, and the joy out of you. They're feeding you what they are.

The good news is, you don't have to live with bitter roots. Ask God to show you what's causing you to be bitter. Maybe you need to forgive somebody, or maybe you're still sour about a dream that didn't work out, or maybe you're still beating yourself up over a mistake you made. Be honest with yourself and say, "God, help me to get rid of this root of bitterness.

I'm still angry over what happened when I was ten years old, still sour over the person who left me. I'm still grieving over my

> *The good news is, you don't have to live with bitter roots.*

loved one whom I lost many years ago. God, I don't want to be bitter. I want my passion back. I want to love again. I want to dream again. God, help me to let it go and move up to the next level."

That's the first step to getting rid of a bitter root. Find out what it is and ask God to help you. You can't do it on your own. Ask Him to help you forgive the person who hurt you. Ask Him to help you release the bitterness and the resentment. When you get those contaminants out, you'll not only feel the weight lift off you, but you'll get your joy back. You'll start dreaming again, and you'll see the new things God has in store for you.

Be Contaminant-Free

Years ago there was a severe outbreak of disease in a small village in Africa. People were being overcome by nausea and sickness, and after a couple of months it was so bad that people started to die. Word quickly reached officials in the main city in the region, and they sent out experts to find out what the problem was. After several days of testing the water from the mountain stream where this little village got its water, they discovered the water was contaminated. The researchers traveled upstream for days and days to find out what and where the problem was, but they didn't see anything wrong. When they finally came to the source of the stream, everything looked fine on the surface. They decided to send divers down to get as close to the stream's source as possible. Much to their surprise, they found that a big mother pig and all her piglets had somehow fallen in and drowned right at the source and had become wedged at the opening. Now all the crystal-clear water was being contaminated as it flowed past the dead pigs. Once they removed the pigs, the water was perfectly fine.

It's the same principle in our lives. We all have unfair things that happen, things we don't understand. Too often, instead of forgiving the people who hurt us, instead of letting go of the wrong, we've held on to it and, like those pigs, it's contaminated our stream. You wonder why you're negative, why you can't get along in relationships, why you keep losing your temper. You come to think, *This is just who I am,* but that is not who you are. You were created in the image of God. He made you to be happy, healthy, whole, and secure—not bitter, angry, and resentful.

You need to go back and get rid of whatever is contaminating your stream. You need to forgive the people who did you wrong. They hurt you once; don't let them continue to hurt you. They can't stop your destiny unless you allow them to. You're not forgiving for their sake. You're forgiving for your sake, so your stream doesn't stay polluted. Quit reliving the dream that didn't work out, the business that failed, the contract that didn't go through. Let it go. God has another dream. That was a test. You had to experience those closed doors before you could come to your open doors. It may not have been fair, but God saw what happened. If you'll get rid of the

> *You need to go back and get rid of whatever is contaminating your stream.*

pigs, if you'll turn it over to Him and start dreaming again, start believing again, start hoping again, God will pay you back for what didn't work out. He's going to open doors to new levels you never dreamed would open. He's going to bring people to you who are better than you ever imagined. What's in your future is much greater than anything you've lost.

Don't let a dead pig keep you from your destiny. Don't let a bitter root contaminate your life. It's time to move forward. It's very freeing when you can let things go and say, "God, they did me wrong, but You are my vindicator. I had a disappointment, but I know that You'll turn what was meant for my harm and use it to my advantage. I lost a loved one, and, yes, I still miss them, but I'm not going to live bitter the rest of my life. You have a new beginning for me." That's how you beat bitterness: You guard your heart. You don't let what's on the outside get on the inside.

Don't Change Your Name

In the Scripture, a lady named Naomi had some tough times. She was living outside of Israel in the country of Moab. She was a widow who had lost her husband, and then, years later, both of her married sons also died. Sometimes life doesn't seem fair. You can have more than your share of bad breaks. It's easy to get bitter and give up on your dreams, but God wouldn't allow it if it was going to keep you from your destiny. Yes, it's difficult, but God promises He will give you grace for every season. He won't let you go through more than you can handle. When that bitterness comes, you have to put your foot down and say, "I'm not going there. I know that God is still in control. I know that His plans for me are for good." What you're going through may not be good, but God knows how to bring good out of it. Every thought will tell you, *It's never going to get better. You may as well be bitter,* but don't believe those lies. You wouldn't be alive unless God has something amazing in front of you. He has a purpose for you to fulfill.

Naomi had gone through so much and was so discouraged she didn't think she could go on. She even changed her name from Naomi, which means "my joy," to Mara, which means "bitter." Then when people called her Naomi, she would tell them, "Don't call me that. Call me Mara. I'm bitter. I'm broken. My dreams are shattered. Just let me live in my pain."

> *Just because you've been through loss doesn't mean you're not going to win again.*

She let the bitterness get on the inside. Sure, she had a reason and had suffered through a lot of losses, but just because you've been through loss doesn't mean you're not going to win again. It doesn't mean you've seen your best days. You may have had bad breaks, but don't change your name. God is not finished with you. The enemy doesn't have the final say; God does.

Naomi moved back to her former home in Bethlehem, and her daughter-in-law Ruth went with her. I can imagine when Naomi's friends saw her, they came running out of their houses and exclaimed, "Naomi, we can't believe it's you!" She replied, "Don't be happy for me. I went out full, but I'm coming home empty." She was saying, "I went out with my husband and my two sons, but now it's just me."

Have you ever gone out full, with big dreams and big goals, but things didn't work out the way you had planned? The marriage didn't make it, the pregnancy failed, the contract didn't go through. As it was with Naomi, you could easily be bitter. Here's how merciful God is. Even though Naomi thought she was done, even though she gave up on her dreams, God said, in effect, "Naomi, you started in joy, and you're going to finish in joy. You may have changed your name, but I didn't change your name. You had trouble in Moab, but I have a blessing waiting for you in Bethlehem."

What's interesting is that even though Naomi changed her name, the Scripture never refers to her as Mara. It keeps calling her Naomi. Have you changed your name, so to speak, to Mara? Are you living bitter and negative, thinking and rethinking about everything that didn't work out? Do yourself a favor. Get rid of those names you've put on yourself and go back to being who God created you to be. God didn't change your name. He still calls you blessed, prosperous, favored, healthy, strong, and victorious. Go back to your original name. You may have had trouble in Moab, but get ready. God has a blessing waiting for you in Bethlehem, right where you are.

Instead of sitting around feeling bitter, Naomi started helping her widowed daughter-in-law Ruth. There was a man whom Ruth was interested in, and

Naomi started giving her relationship advice. She told Ruth, "Put on this perfume and wear this outfit, then go see this man named Boaz." Naomi turned her focus away from her own problems and started helping somebody else. When she did, her joy began to come back. When you're tempted to be bitter, one of the best things you can do is to get your mind off your-

> *When you're tempted to be bitter, one of the best things you can do is to get your mind off yourself and go be a blessing to others.*

self and go be a blessing to others. Ruth ended up marrying Boaz, and they had a baby named Obed. When Naomi saw that little baby, she was so excited. It was as though something breathed new life, a new sense of purpose, back into her spirit. The Scripture says, "A son was born to Naomi." It wasn't even her baby, but she took that little baby and raised him as though he was her own. This once bitter woman was now more fulfilled than ever. She never dreamed she could be that happy again. God is saying, "My blessing is going to override your bitterness. My favor is going to make up for your pain." What God has planned for you cannot be stopped by people, by bad breaks, by loss. Even if you change your name, God is so merciful that He's still going to do something amazing. He's still going to get you to where you're supposed to be.

Not "Here" but "There"

In Mark 16, Jesus had been crucified and His body was laid in a tomb. Mary Magdalene, another Mary who was the mother of James, and a woman named Salome went to the tomb early the next morning to put perfume on His body. They wondered how they were going to roll the stone away from the entrance to the tomb, but when they arrived, the stone was already moved. They walked into the tomb and saw a young man dressed in a white robe. It was an angel, which frightened them. He said to them, "You're looking for Jesus, but He is not here. He has risen! He is going ahead of you into Galilee. There you will see Him." Notice that the angel said, "He is not *here*. He is *there*." The angel was saying, in effect, "I know this looks bad. I know you're hurting. I know you're disappointed, but don't stay here. Something better is waiting for you there."

In other words, "here" is the disappointment. "Here" is the bad medical report. "Here" is the dream that didn't work out. If you stay "here," you'll be discouraged. You have to go "there." Sometimes the reason God doesn't comfort us in the "here," in the disappointment, is because He doesn't want us to stay where we are. Yes, the loss is painful. Yes, the setback wasn't fair, but God is not "here." He's gone ahead. He's waiting for you "there." God is not in your past, in what you lost, in what didn't work out. He's in your future. Don't get stuck in "here." Move forward into "there." "There" is where the vindication is. "There" is where new beginnings are. "There" is where you'll find your healing. If these three ladies had stayed at the tomb in self-pity, saying, "We can't believe this happened," they would never have seen the "there." They would never have seen the Lord.

> *God is not in your past, in what you lost, in what didn't work out. He's in your future.*

Are you living in the "here," while God is waiting for you "there"? Are you stuck in a disappointment, bitter over a bad break, angry over what didn't work out? It's time to leave "here" and go "there." "There" is where God is waiting for you. "There" is where the blessing is. The disappointment is simply a season. It's not the rest of your life. God has already gone ahead. God has already lined up the next chapter, the next level. Your house was damaged in the storm. That's "here." Yes, that's disappointing. The good news is, God has gone ahead. He's waiting for you "there." He has restoration already lined up.

This is what my father had to do. He'd been pastoring a church for many years, and he was very successful. They had just built a beautiful new sanctuary. He was on the state board for his denomination, on his way up. Then my sister Lisa was born with something like cerebral palsy, and my dad began to search the Scripture in a new way. He found how God is a healer and how Jesus came that we might live an abundant, victorious life. He started sharing this good news with his congregation, but, much to his surprise, they didn't like his new message of faith and victory and healing. It didn't fit in their denominational teaching back then. People whom my father had known for years suddenly turned on him. Lifelong friends of my parents wouldn't speak to either of them anymore. My father ended up having to leave that church. He was so disappointed. He never dreamed he'd have to start all over. He could have been bitter and said, "God, why did You let this happen? I was being my best. I was honoring You." Like Mary, he was in the "here." He didn't understand it, and, yes, the "here" wasn't fair, but what he couldn't see was that God had already gone ahead. God had already lined up Lakewood and was waiting for him "there." If my father had stayed in the "here," he would have missed his destiny. He left that church and started Lakewood with ninety people. That was over fifty years ago, and we are still going strong.

What am I saying? The "here" is not the end. The disappointment, the loss, and the betrayal are temporary. God has already gone ahead. Don't let bitterness hold you back. Don't sit around in self-pity. Move forward into "there." "There" is where God will pay you back. "There" is where He'll do more than you can ask or think of.

> *The "here" is not the end. The disappointment, the loss, and the betrayal are temporary.*

Come into the Party

In Chapter Six, I wrote about the prodigal son and how, after he left home with his father's inheritance and made poor choices, his father came running out to meet him and welcome him back home with open arms. The father was so glad to have his son back that he told his staff to go kill the fatted calf and have a feast and celebrate with a party. However, the older brother was out in the field working at the time. When he heard all the music and the dancing, he asked one of the staff what the celebration was all about. They told him, "Your brother has come home. Your father is celebrating his safe return with a party to welcome him back." The Scripture says, "The older brother became angry and refused to go in." So his father went out and pleaded with him, "Come on, son. Come in. Your brother is back home." The older brother replied, "Dad, I've been slaving away for you all these years and have always done what you asked. But you've never even given me a skinny goat, and now you go and kill a fatted calf for him, even after all the bad things he's done." You can hear the bitterness in his spirit. He's saying,

"It's not fair. You haven't treated me right. I'm not coming into your party."

Here's my point: The party went on without him. His bitterness didn't stop the party; it just kept him from going into the party. Sometimes we're holding on to unforgiveness, anger, and resentment, thinking that it's hurting the other person. The truth is, the party is still going on. It's only hurting us. Are you letting bitterness keep you out of the party? Are you letting a disappointment keep you from enjoying today? Why don't you let it go and come into the party? Life is happening, there's a celebration going on. Today is a gift. Don't let a bad childhood keep you out of the party. Don't let a divorce or a breakup cause you to be sour and sit on the sidelines of life. Come into the party.

> *Are you letting a disappointment keep you from enjoying today?*

Start dreaming again. Start loving again. Start believing again. We have no guarantee that we're going to be here tomorrow. Life is fragile. Time is too short for you to live offended and in bitterness, in self-pity. God knows what you didn't get. Quit trying to get people to pay you back; go to God, and He'll make it up to you. If you'll come into the party, if you'll get rid of what's contaminating you, I believe and declare that every root of bitterness is coming up right now. You're going to experience a new sense of freedom, better relationships, greater joy, and clearer vision. You're going to rise higher, live happier, and reach the fullness of your destiny.

CHAPTER TEN

Remove the Shame

Starting in our childhoods, we've all heard the phrase "Shame on you." When you didn't clean your room, you were told, "Shame on you." When you were mean to your little brother or sister, once again it was, "Shame on you." Even as adults, we might not hear the words spoken out loud to us, but they still play over and over in our thoughts. If you fell back into a bad habit, you told yourself, "Shame on you." If you went through a divorce, the message was repeated over and over: "Shame on you." We don't realize how destructive shame is. We use it to try to convince people to do better, but shame does just the opposite. It causes us to feel guilty and unworthy, as though we don't deserve to be blessed.

A young lady told me that when she was a teenager

she had a baby whom she wasn't able to keep, so she put the baby up for adoption. Now, ten years later, she said, "I feel so ashamed for abandoning my baby. I can't sleep at night thinking about what a terrible mother I am." There is a voice that is constantly whispering to her, "Shame on you." Shame is one of the enemy's favorite tools. He is called "the accuser," and he will remind you of every mistake and every failure you've ever made, even about things that weren't your fault. He'll try to deceive you into thinking that you were to blame. To people who were abused as children, who were innocent victims of it, he'll whisper, "You're not good enough. You deserved it. That's why they mistreated you." He'll try to twist it and convince you to carry around all this heaviness.

But the Scripture speaks of how God has removed our shame. Whether it was your fault or somebody else's fault, you don't have to carry the heavy load of guilt, or beat yourself up over past mistakes, or feel wrong on the inside. When the enemy says, "Shame on you," God says, "Shame off you. I've forgiven you. I've redeemed you. I've made you valuable." Whatever people did or didn't do to you, they don't determine your worth. Your worth comes from your Creator. The Most High God breathed His life into you. He crowned you with His favor. He calls you a masterpiece. Don't go around feeling ashamed, guilty, and condemned. Shake off the shame. Every time you hear that voice whispering, "Shame on you," by faith you need to hear God answering back, "Shame off you!" Don't accept the shame. I'm not saying to be flippant and think, *I made a big mistake. I hurt somebody, but it's no big deal.* When we have done wrong to someone, we should be remorseful toward them, ask them for forgiveness, and determine to do better next time. But the problem is that if you don't put your foot down and say, "Shame off me," that shame will follow you around even though God has removed it.

The young lady who gave up her baby asked me, "Joel, do you think God will forgive me?" I said, "I know God will forgive you. The real question is, Will you forgive yourself? Will you shake off the shame?" I have found that it is more difficult to forgive ourselves than it is to forgive other people. The enemy knows that if we feel wrong on the inside, we'll never become who we were created to be. That's why he works overtime to try to bring guilt and shame on you, to make you feel as though you don't deserve to be blessed. You have to turn off the accusing voices. Next level thinking says you may have made mistakes, but the moment you asked God to forgive you, He not only forgave you but He took it one step further and doesn't even remember it anymore. Those condemning thoughts try to remind you of your past mistakes, saying things such as, "Shame on you for being unfaithful in that relationship. Shame on you for being dishonest in the business deal. Shame on you for being rude to your family member last month." You've already asked for forgiveness, which means that God doesn't remember it. That voice is a sure sign the accuser is at work. You can either accept the shame and feel wrong on the inside, or you can rise up and say, "No, shame off me! I know I've been forgiven. I know God's mercy is bigger than this mistake. If God doesn't remember it, I'm not going to remember it either."

> *The real question is, Will you forgive yourself? Will you shake off the shame?*

The Reproach Has Been Rolled Away

During the hundreds of years when the Israelites were slaves in Egypt, they were very beaten down, not only physically but emotionally. They were constantly told that they were no good, that they couldn't do anything right, that they would never measure up, and that they deserved to be punished. Over time the Israelites let that steal their sense of value. They felt inferior and insecure, as though they had no self-worth. When a person is being mistreated and abused, especially for a long time, instead of recognizing that the other person is doing them wrong, it's easy for them to accept the blame and start thinking they deserve what's happening. Before long they're ashamed not only of what's happening to them, but they also start to become ashamed of who they are. That's the way the Israelites felt. But after 430 years of enduring it, God brought them out of the slavery, out of the abuse. As they were approaching the Promised Land, God said to them, "This day I have rolled away the reproach of Egypt from you." The word *reproach* means "shame, blame, disgrace." They couldn't go into the Promised Land with the shame of feeling unworthy and not valuable. God had to roll the reproach off them.

In the same way, before you can reach your highest potential, you have to get rid of any shame. You may have made mistakes and other people may have done you wrong. But you can't sit around feeling guilty and condemned, blaming yourself and blaming others. Whatever your Egypt is—a divorce, or an addiction, or somebody who did you wrong—God is saying, "This day—not tomorrow, not next week, not six months from now, but today—I am rolling away the reproach." He's rolling away the guilt and the shame. Now it's up to you to accept it. You have to quit dwelling on your failures. Quit believing the lies that you've made too many

> *Before you can reach your highest potential, you have to get rid of any shame.*

mistakes or that you've been hurt too badly. The reproach has been rolled away. When you get up in the morning and you hear that voice saying, "Shame on you," answer right back, "No, shame off me! I know my reproach has been taken away."

Don't Let Your Past Become Your Identity

I know a man who was happily married and had
a good family, but he let his guard down and got
involved with another woman. They had been friends
at work, but in the heat of the moment it turned into
something wrong. It happened one time, and that was
it. He knew it was wrong and felt so badly about
it. He asked God to forgive him, but year after year
went by and he continued to feel a heaviness inside.
He knew God had forgiven him, but he couldn't
forgive himself. On the outside he looked fine; he
seemed happy. But on the inside he carried a sense
of shame and guilt, as though he had to settle for
second best. One day a minister whom he respected
pulled him to the side and said, "Whatever is holding you back, whatever lie is keeping you from rising
higher, today that power is being broken! God is
about to release you to a new level of your destiny!"
This man began to weep and weep. All the guilt, all
the shame, and all the heaviness that he had allowed
to become a part of his life suddenly lifted off him.
It was as though a chain was broken, as though a
stronghold had been torn down. For years he had

allowed the accuser to pile on the shame and tell him, "You don't deserve forgiveness. You blew it, so sit on the sidelines in your shame." God showed up and said, "I have the final say, and I say shame off you!" In that moment he was changed.

Maybe like him, you know God has forgiven you, but you still have a sense of unworthiness as though you don't deserve it. Perhaps you've become convinced that you can never reach your highest potential. Friend, that shame has held you back long enough. Today God has removed the reproach. Today the chains have been broken. Burdens have been lifted. God is saying, "Shame off you!" Now you have to get in agreement with Him. Quit listening to the accusing voices. Quit believing the lies that you have to settle for second best. Nothing you've done was a surprise to God. He's not up in heaven scratching His head and saying, "Oh, man, I didn't see that last mistake coming. It threw me off." God's mercy was there for you before you made the mistake. He had the solution before you had the problem. It's time for you to shake off the shame, to

> *Quit believing the lies that you have to settle for second best.*

shake off the guilt. This is a new day. The reproach has been rolled away.

Don't let negative events from your past become your identity. Don't let a failure, a divorce, a bankruptcy, or an addiction become who you are. It's easy to take all the blame and then let it consume you with guilt. Before long you'll become known as the man who blew his marriage, or the woman who was abused, or the young person who has the addiction. That's what you did; that's not who you are. That's what happened to you; that is not your identity. The enemy would love to stick labels on us, such as addicted, unfaithful, divorced, or bad parent. Don't believe those lies. You may struggle with an addiction, but you are not an addict. What you do does not change your identity. You are still a child of the Most High God. You may have failed in some area of your life—we all have—but you're not a failure. You may have had some bad breaks, but you are not a victim. When those thoughts of guilt and shame try to label you, you have to remind yourself, "I am not who people say I am. I am not who circumstances say I am. I am who God says I am. He says I am approved, I am accepted, I am valuable, and I am a masterpiece."

Time for a Name Change

In the Scripture, names were given a lot more meaning and significance than they are today. Isaac had a son whom he named Jacob. *Jacob* means "a supplanter, one who is a trickster, a swindler, a deceiver." Every time someone said, "Hello, Jacob!" they were saying, "Hello, trickster!" "Good morning, Jacob. Good morning, con man." "It's time to go to school, Jacob. It's time to go to school, cheater." He had heard this for so long that he didn't know any better. He became exactly what people called him. After years of being told, "You're a con man," he conned his brother, Esau, out of his inheritance. He was told over and over again, "You're a cheater," and he cheated his uncle and went around tricking other people.

Genesis 32 records that later in Jacob's life, he got tired of living like that and decided to return with his family to his parents' home. One night on the journey back, he went down to the brook to get alone with God, where an angel appeared to him in the form of a man. The angel asked Jacob what his name was, and he responded, "I am Jacob." He was saying, "I am a cheater. I am a deceiver. I am dishonest." The angel didn't say, "You're right, Jacob. You've lived a really terrible life, and you should be ashamed of yourself." Rather, the angel said, "Your name will no longer be Jacob; your name will be Israel." The name *Israel* means "prince with God." He was saying, "You are not a deceiver. You may have let people talk you into living like that, but that is not your true identity. God has a new name for you. You are a prince." God took this man who had lived a dishonest life of cheating others, and instead of giving him what he deserved, instead of shaking His finger and saying, "Shame on you, Jacob," God said, "Shame

> *The angel didn't say, "You're right, Jacob. You've lived a really terrible life, and you should be ashamed of yourself."*

off you, Jacob. You're My son. I have destined you to leave your mark on your generation, and not in disgrace or as a failure. I've called you to be a prince. I've called you to reign in life." The first thing God had to do was remove the reproach. God had to get the shame off Jacob.

Maybe, like Jacob, you are wearing negative labels

today. Have you let your circumstances, your failures, or even other people put a label on you that says "not valuable, not worthy, addicted, bad parent, blew his marriage, doesn't deserve to be blessed"? No, this is what grace is all about. None of us deserve it, but God says, "I'm going to bless you anyway. I know your true identity. I've breathed My life into you." You may feel like Jacob—you've made poor choices and could easily live with a sense of shame. But God is changing our names today to "Prince," to "Princess," to "Redeemed," to "Forgiven," to "Highly Favored." Jacob could have easily told the angel, "I don't see how God could ever make me a prince. I've made so many bad choices." Instead he accepted it into his spirit. He agreed with what God said. In fact, Jacob had told the angel, "I'm not letting you go until you bless me!" He was saying, "I might not deserve it, but since the shame has been rolled away, I'm asking for favor. I'm asking for new levels. I'm asking for the fullness of my destiny." God didn't say, "Jacob, who do you think you are? I'm not going to bless you. You know the life you've lived." Rather, God said, "Jacob, I like your boldness. I like the fact that you shook off the shame. You got rid of the guilt. Now you're ready to step up to who I've created you to be." When you make that decision, God will bless you in amazing ways.

Healing Begins When We Get Honest

If you're still struggling in an area today, there is no shame in asking for help. Sometimes we think we're supposed to be perfect, so we can't let anybody know we have a bad habit, an addiction, or a struggle. We would be embarrassed if others knew. Don't let shame keep you isolated. Real healing begins when we get honest. The Scripture says, "Confess your faults to one another and pray for one another so that you may be healed." There are some things that you can't overcome on your own. You need somebody to stand in faith with you. I'm not saying you have to announce your struggle to others, but you can find a

> *Don't let shame keep you isolated.*

person of integrity whom you can trust to walk with you through it. There's something about getting it out in the open. Don't let the fear of what other people think keep you from your miracle. I've learned that everybody is dealing with something. The people who you think have it all together, who always look fine on the outside, they're good at pretending. Everyone has issues.

It's easy to hide things in our lives and let people see only what we want them to see. Even in the Scripture, all the heroes of faith had their weaknesses. One day Peter was cursing people out, denying that he knew Jesus. Weeks later he was telling a crippled man to rise and walk and preaching to thousands. One day David was defeating a giant and leading God's people to a great victory. On another day he was committing adultery and having the lady's husband killed. He was so ashamed of himself that he tried to hide it for a year. Finally David was confronted by the prophet Nathan, and he got it out in the open, confessed his faults, and God restored him. One day Noah was building the ark by faith, saving his family from the Flood. On another day he was drunk on the floor of his tent. You think you have things to be ashamed of?

Many times the things you're struggling with didn't start with you. They were passed down. Now this is your opportunity to put an end to it. You can be the one to break the negative cycle in your family. The first step is to shake off the shame. Don't be embarrassed. Don't try to hide it. You don't have to go through life pretend-ing. If you'll be honest, go to God and ask Him for help, find a friend to walk it out with you, then you can overcome anything that's holding you back. The forces for you are greater than the forces against you.

> *You don't have to go through life pretending.*

I received a letter from a teenage girl who told how she struggled with anorexia. She would hardly eat anything and got to the point where she was down to skin and bones. On top of that, she was cutting herself. That seemed to be the only way she could find relief from the pain she felt on the inside. She came from a well-respected family and was too embarrassed to tell anyone. She felt ashamed of who she was, and she was overwhelmed with guilt for injuring herself. She knew it was wrong, but she kept hearing the voices say, "You're not valuable. You're no good. Look at you and what you've done to yourself." That's what the enemy loves to do—heap on the guilt and the shame. He knows it will keep us from our destiny. She got to the point where she was so beaten down that she wouldn't look anyone in the eyes. One day she heard me talking about how God will heal your hurts, how He'll give you beauty for ashes, and how there's no shame in being honest and going to God and asking for help. That day she made the decision that she wasn't going to pretend anymore. She told her parents what was going on. They got her the help she needed. Today she's not only healthy, whole, and free, but she's a counselor who is helping other young people who are struggling with the same issues.

That's what happens when you shake off the shame. God will take your scars and turn them into stars. He'll use you to help others. Maybe you're struggling in an area right now. The next time you hear that voice whispering, "Shame on you," instead of believing that lie, beating yourself up, and getting depressed, rise up and declare, "No, shame off me!" If you'll start shaking off the guilt and the shame, you can enter into your Promised Land. That's when you'll see the healing, the breakthrough, and the new levels.

Payback Is Coming

Some people are living with a sense of shame because of something that happened to them that wasn't even their fault. You might have been mistreated when you were growing up. Somebody took advantage of you. The enemy will twist things and try to convince you that it was your fault. Don't believe those lies. If they did you wrong, the problem wasn't with you; the problem was with them. God saw what happened. He saw the injustice. You may think, *Nobody knows what I've endured. Nobody knows my hurts, my shame, my pains.* But God knows. He saw every person who lifted a finger against you. He saw every lonely night, every tear, and every hurt. God said in Isaiah 54, "You will forget the shame of your youth. You will not remember the reproach." God is going to pay you back for the injustices in such a way that you won't even remember what happened. It's not going to be on the forefront of your mind. He's going to make your life so blessed, so rewarding, and so fulfilling that you won't even think about the people who hurt you.

Now do your part and forgive the people who did you wrong. As long as you continue to dwell on it, you're allowing them to continue to hurt you. Let it go. What they have done to you did not change your identity. You're still a masterpiece. You're still wearing a crown of favor. You're still destined to do great things. You need to take off the old labels that say "Damaged," "Mistreated," or "Abused." Put on some new labels, such as "Accepted," "Approved," "Valuable," and "Masterpiece." When you do that, God promises that you will not only forget the shame of your past, but He takes it a step further. He says in Isaiah 61, "Instead of your former shame you shall receive a twofold recompense. Instead of dishonor and reproach you will possess double what you forfeited." You may have had some unfair things happen, but stay in faith. Because of the injustice, God is going to pay you back double. God saw when the person walked out and broke your heart. He saw the people who mistreated you and made you feel ashamed. Nothing went unnoticed. He's going to pay you back with double the joy, double the peace, double the honor, and double the fulfillment. Your life is going to be richer because of the injustices.

> *As long as you continue to dwell on it, you're allowing them to continue to hurt you. Let it go.*

This promise won't do us any good, however, if we sit back feeling ashamed and guilty and are beating ourselves up. Put your shoulders back and hold your head high. Nothing that was done to you, and nothing that you have done, has changed your identity. You are still a child of the Most High God. His plans for you are still for good and not evil. You may have had some bad breaks, but really those setbacks were a setup for God to bring you out with double.

Reprogram Your Thinking

I know a lady who always struggled with her self-worth. Growing up, she never felt as though she was good enough. This insecurity came from being born out of wedlock. Her mother and father weren't married. When she was a child, she saw a little checked box on her birth certificate that said "Illegitimate." That word became ingrained in her thinking. All through her childhood and her teenage years, she felt inferior. Anytime she tried to move forward, she would hear voices whispering, "You weren't wanted. You're not valuable. There's something wrong with you." She went around with a sense of shame and unworthiness. She was wearing the labels "Illegiti-mate" and "Not Up to Par." One day she heard me talking about how our worth and value doesn't come from people; it comes from God. She said, "It was as though something exploded on the inside." Instead of believing the lies that told her she should be ashamed, that she has no value, she started reprogramming her thinking by telling herself, *I am not an accident. I am not a mistake. I have been handpicked by Almighty God. I am fearfully and wonderfully made.* Her atti-tude was, *No matter what my birth certificate says, I know I am legitimate. The Most High God breathed His life into me.* Today she is living a free, blessed, confident, faith-filled life. Just as God promised, she doesn't remember the shame of her youth.

Are you carrying around guilt, shame, and heavi-ness? This is your day to be set free! The reproach has been rolled away. The door is open, but you have to walk out. Take off the negative labels. When the enemy whis-pers, "Shame on you," answer right back, "No, shame off me. I've been

> *When the enemy whispers, "Shame on you," answer right back, "No, shame off me."*

forgiven. I've been redeemed. I am valuable." If you do this, I believe and declare God is going to pay you back double for that injustice. You're going to enter into your Promised Land and reach the fullness of your destiny.

ACKNOWLEDGMENTS

In this book I offer many stories shared with me by friends, members of our congregation, and people I've met around the world. I appreciate and acknowledge their contributions and support. Some of those mentioned in the book are people I have not met personally, and in a few cases, we've changed the names to protect the privacy of individuals. I give honor to all those to whom honor is due. As the son of a church leader and a pastor myself, I've listened to countless sermons and presentations, so in some cases I can't remember the exact source of a story.

I am indebted to the amazing staff of Lakewood Church, the wonderful members of Lakewood who share their stories with me, and those around the world who generously support our ministry and make it possible to bring hope to a world in need. I am grateful to all of those who follow our services on television, the Internet, SiriusXM, and through the podcasts. You are all part of our Lakewood family.

I offer special thanks also to all the pastors across the country who are members of our Champions Network.

Once again, I am grateful for a wonderful team of professionals who helped me put this book together for you. Leading them is my FaithWords/Hachette publisher, Rolf Zettersten, along with team members Patsy Jones, Billy Clark, and Hannah Phillips. I truly appreciate the editorial contributions of wordsmith Lance Wubbels.

I am grateful also to my literary agents Jan Miller Rich and Shannon Marven at Dupree Miller & Associates.

And last but not least, thanks to my wife, Victoria, and our children, Jonathan and Alexandra, who are my sources of daily inspiration, as well as our closest family members, who serve as day-to-day leaders of our ministry, including my mother, Dodie; my brother, Paul, and his wife, Jennifer; my sister Lisa and her husband, Kevin; and my brother-in-law Don and his wife, Jackelyn.

We Want to Hear from You!

Each week, I close our international television broadcast by giving the audience an opportunity to make Jesus the Lord of their lives. I'd like to extend that same opportunity to you.

Are you at peace with God? A void exists in every person's heart that only God can fill. I'm not talking about joining a church or finding religion. I'm talking about finding life and peace and happiness. Would you pray with me today? Just say, "Lord Jesus, I repent of my sins. I ask You to come into my heart. I make You my Lord and Savior."

Friend, if you prayed that simple prayer, I believe you have been "born again." I encourage you to attend a good Bible-based church and keep God in first place in your life. For free information on how you can grow stronger in your spiritual life, please feel free to contact us.

Victoria and I love you, and we'll be praying for you. We're believing for God's best for you, that you will see your dreams come to pass. We'd love to hear from you!

To contact us, write to:

Joel and Victoria Osteen
P.O. Box 4600
Houston, TX 77210

Or you can reach us online at www.joelosteen.com.

Stay connected, be blessed.

From thoughtful articles to powerful blogs, podcasts and more, JoelOsteen.com is full of inspirations that will give you encouragement and confidence in your daily life.

Visit us today at JoelOsteen.com.

Hope is on the move!

Watch messages, read our free daily devotional and more! Inspiration is always at your fingertips with the free Joel Osteen app for iPhone and Android.

Thanks for helping us make a difference in the lives of millions around the world.